PETER GORDON'S WORLD KITCHEN

Photography by Jean Cazals

TEN SPEED PRESS
Berkeley | Toronto

1⊖

Ten Speed Press
Box 7123
Berkeley, California 94707
www.tenspeed.com

Distributed in Canada by Ten Speed Press Canada.

Cover design by Betsy Stromberg
Interior design by Hodder Moa Beckett Publishers Ltd.
Photographs supplied by *New Zealand House & Garden*
Production work on U.S. edition by Betsy Stromberg

Library of Congress Cataloging-in-Publication Data
on file with the publisher.
ISBN-10: 1-58008-679-9
ISBN-13: 978-1-58008-679-0

Originally published in New Zealand by
Hodder Moa Beckett Publishers Ltd.

Printed in China

First printing of U.S. edition 2005

1 2 3 4 5 6 7 8 9 10 — 09 08 07 06 05

contents

I'd like to thank the editors at *New Zealand House & Garden* for giving me a platform to write these recipes over the past seven years. It has been a great relationship, and I'm very proud of what we have achieved.

Also, a big thank you to the team at Hodder Moa Beckett, who enthusiastically helped these recipes to print.

Passion fruit panna cotta, page 196

introduction

Someone recently asked me how my food has changed over the years. I'd have to answer that as my shopping list of potential ingredients has increased the more I've traveled, so has the potential for mixing ingredients in harmony. However, the one thing that has remained constant in my cooking is a desire that flavor and texture be the pivotal characteristics. I have stages when I realize I've been on a bit of a Turkish bent (I consult for a restaurant in Istanbul called *changa* and go there frequently) or stuck on a Japanese theme for a while, then decide I should head back to the mixing grounds. Where an ingredient is grown isn't important to me. That I marinate New Zealand lamb in a mix of Thai chile and Japanese mirin, then serve it on grilled Spanish artichokes and Jersey Royals doesn't bother me in the slightest. There are many chefs cooking beautiful, authentic regional food, but I'm not interested in such a pursuit—I love to eat it, but I don't want to cook it. I cook what excites me, and the world as a whole excites me more than a region defined by political boundaries.

What does concern me is that the produce I use is grown or raised properly, with good animal husbandry and few, if any, pesticides or genetic modifications. Although I'm lucky to be able to get excellent organic meat and vegetables, I mostly eat fantastic, traditionally farmed produce, where organic isn't an option for the farmers, but they do their best to produce food in harmony with the environment. Choosing what we eat is important, and we need to lead the way by insisting on good-quality produce at little cost to the Earth.

This book has been produced because for over seven years I've been writing for one of New Zealand's best magazines, *New Zealand House & Garden*, which few people outside New Zealand will have seen. That doesn't seem fair to me, as I have written over 200 recipes for the magazine, and I'd like to share them. In *Peter Gordon's World Kitchen,* you'll find some delicious recipes that I'd hate to think would remain unknown—that is, unless you've been to the restaurant I co-own in London, The Providores. We have numerous copies of *New Zealand House & Garden* for our guests to read in the Tapa Room as they have their caffé lattes and breakfast in the morning, their beet risotto for lunch, and their crispy roast pork belly and a glass of New Zealand pinot noir in the evening. The Providores and Tapa Room, to give it its full title, opened in August 2001, and it has been our baby ever since. I co-own it with my partner, Michael McGrath (who inspired me to get this book together); Anna Hansen; and Jeremy Leeming. Anna and I run the kitchen together, and Michael and Jeremy look after behind-the-scenes management. We have a great team working with us, and in many ways, their ethnic variety reflects the fusion food we cook, from people such as our Venezuelan manager, Otto Lauterbach, through to kitchen staff and waiters from Somalia, Poland, Argentina, Spain, Australia, New Zealand, and the rest of the globe.

My column in *New Zealand House & Garden* came about in 1996, when I wrote to then-editor Liz Parker, asking if I could write a recipe column for the magazine. She took me on, and it's been a great relationship with the magazine ever since. Liz moved on and was replaced by Kate Coughlin, and under her, the magazine has become even more glossy and beautiful. My current boss at the magazine, who is great fun, is food editor Sally Butters, who has guided me through various story ideas and recipe testings.

During these seven years, I've spent one weekend day every two to three months with my friend Jean Cazals, cooking the dishes that appear in the magazine and now here also in this book. Jean is not only the photographer but also the food stylist—he has a huge appreciation and love of food. We tend to get to the point, after we've shot a few dishes, when we start wondering in which order we should eat them. He makes my food look good, and I make sure the recipes will be as clear as possible so that you can make them just as well.

I must emphasize that these recipes have not been written solely for the New Zealand reader, but for cooks the world over. A good recipe isn't geographical in its appeal or approach, but you will find a sense of modern New Zealand throughout the book. Some things, however, may seem peculiarly Kiwi. For example, I frequently use the vegetable "kumara" in this book. It's our native sweet potato (brought across the Pacific by the first waves of Maori to settle in New Zealand over 500 years ago), and to give it another name for reasons of familiarity in another country would seem rude. However, you can replace kumara with sweet potatos or yams. Likewise, the fish we have in New Zealand and Australia will differ slightly from those in the Northern Hemisphere. When you see a recipe for hapuku, you can replace it with grouper; flounder can be replaced by lemon or Dover sole, wild salmon or farmed organic salmon with trout, and Blue cod with farmed

Norwegian cod or line-caught cod. Just promise me you will never overcook it. Well-done fish really isn't worth the effort.

My message for this book is simply to have a good time in the kitchen. Shopping for food can be just as much fun as cooking it, so don't make the shopping trip a bore—turn it into a discovery. There are many great recipes here, all written for the home cook, and if I have been able to throw together eight of them every few months in my or Jean's kitchen, then you will be able to as well.

Happy cooking!

Peter Gordon

Steamed fish and bacon wontons with sweet chile sauce, page 122

light meals, snacks, and starters

These recipes are some of the most common things I cook at home. Sometimes the thought of making a three-course meal for lunch just doesn't appeal! Being a busy chef in the restaurant sometimes means that all I really want to eat when I get home is some toast spread with tahini and honey, or leftover potatoes fried in olive oil with chorizo, or maybe just some cold roast chicken tossed with avocado, avocado oil, arugula, and mayonnaise. Light meals are a favorite of busy people, and they're versatile: a breakfast dish could become a favorite lunch dish or a late supper snack. I've also added a couple of fruity breakfast-type drinks, although the berry punch may make the rest of your day a little hazy!

Melon and avocado breakfast

This could barely be called a recipe, but it's a good, refreshing combination to have up your sleeve. If you can't find pomegranate molasses, use New Zealand manuka honey or another rich honey instead.

Serves 2

- 1 small melon
- 1 large avocado
- 1 lime, halved
- 1 cup thick Greek-style yogurt
- 2 tablespoons pomegranate molasses

Cut melon in half and scoop out and discard seeds. Using a spoon, scoop flesh out of one half and divide between two wide glasses.

Halve avocado and remove pit. Scoop out flesh and place half the avocado in each glass. Scoop remaining flesh from the melon and place in the glasses, then squeeze the lime juice over. Dollop half the yogurt on top of each glass of fruit, then drizzle with the molasses.

Corn and blueberry pancakes

These fall into the American category of breakfast pancakes rather than what a New Zealander would call pancakes, which are much thinner and larger like crêpes. They're great served with bacon and avocado for breakfast or with roast duck or chicken at dinnertime.

Makes 6 to 8

- 1 large corn cob, husk removed, *or* $^1\!/_2$ cup canned corn kernels, drained
- $^2\!/_3$ cup flour
- $2^1\!/_2$ tablespoons polenta
- 2 pinches salt
- $1^1\!/_2$ teaspoons baking powder
- $^1\!/_2$ teaspoon baking soda
- 2 tablespoons superfine sugar
- 1 egg
- $^3\!/_4$ cup buttermilk *or* milk with a squeeze of lemon
- $1^1\!/_2$ tablespoons butter, melted
- $^3\!/_4$ cup blueberries (if frozen, don't thaw before adding to batter)
- maple syrup *or* honey to serve

Hold corn cob vertically and firmly on a cutting board and run a knife downward to cut the kernels from the cob. Be careful as you do this, as you don't want the cob to fly off and to cut yourself. You will need $^1\!/_2$ to $^3\!/_4$ cup of kernels.

Sieve together flour, polenta, salt, baking powder, baking soda, and sugar in a wide bowl and make a well in the center. Lightly whisk egg with buttermilk and mix into dry ingredients, then mix in butter. Add blueberries and corn. Heat and lightly oil a heavy frying pan. Dollop in generous spoonfuls of batter, leaving a space between each pancake, and cook over a moderate heat until golden on the bottom and a little set on top. Gently flip and cook until golden on the other side. Keep warm while you cook the rest. Serve drizzled with maple syrup or honey.

Poached egg on crumbed feta and butternut

I ate something similar to this in Istanbul on my thirty-ninth birthday, and it was fantastic. Whenever I head to Istanbul to do consultancy for the restaurant changa (www.changa-istanbul.com), I always bring home several bags of kirmizi biber. They are just chile flakes, but made from Turkish-grown chiles with an almost oily texture, and they have a flavor reminiscent of the street food of Turkey. If you can't locate them, then simply replace with top-quality chile flakes.

Serves 2

2 eggs

white vinegar

6$^1/_2$ oz feta, sliced into $^1/_2$-inch-thick pieces, patted
   dry on paper

1 tablespoon flour

1 egg yolk, beaten

$^1/_2$ cup fresh breadcrumbs

3 tablespoons butter

$^1/_4$ lb steamed butternut squash, diced

2 tablespoons extra virgin olive oil

$^1/_4$ teaspoon kirmizi biber or chile flakes

1 teaspoon chopped mixed herbs (e.g., rosemary,
   oregano, sage, dill)

Poach eggs in water with a few tablespoons of white vinegar added. While they're cooking, toss the feta slices in flour, then coat in egg yolk, and finally coat with the breadcrumbs. Heat up a medium-sized pan, add most of the butter, and fry the feta on both sides until golden and remove to two plates. Warm the butternut squash in the same pan in the remaining butter and place on the feta. Place one poached egg on top of each pile of butternut squash. Warm oil with chile flakes. Add herbs and heat until sizzling, then pour over each egg.

Deep-fried eggs with chile sauce

These eggs are a great brunch snack—something for guests to have with a Bloody Mary while you're getting the rest of the food ready or the croissants are heating. You'll find these snacks in Thailand and Malaysia. Use one egg per person.

Serves 4

1 scant cup superfine sugar

2 tablespoons water

2 red chiles, finely sliced into rings

1 clove garlic, peeled and finely sliced

$^1/_2$ cup cider vinegar

1 teaspoon salt

oil for frying

4 eggs, soft boiled, cooled in ice water, then peeled
   and patted dry

1 small handful cilantro leaves

Place sugar and water in a small saucepan and stir well as you heat. Bring to a boil and add chiles and garlic. Simmer until sugar is slightly caramelized (golden), then add vinegar and salt and bring to a boil. Remove from heat.

Fill a small pan with 2 inches of oil. Heat to around 350°F (the usual deep-frying temperature), then carefully add eggs—off a slotted spoon is a good idea. Fry for around 1$^1/_2$ minutes, until golden, then remove with a slotted spoon and drain. To serve, cut the egg in half (or leave it whole as a surprise), spoon warm chile sauce around it, and sprinkle with cilantro.

Smoked salmon on rösti with minted crème fraîche

Where would brunch be without smoked salmon? This recipe is a good way to use up leftover potatoes, although it's so good you'll possibly want to cook some spuds just to make it.

Serves 2

**about 1 lb potatoes, boiled or roasted in their
   skins, cooled**

1 egg

1 small red onion, peeled and finely sliced

1 scant teaspoon salt

1 scant teaspoon freshly ground pepper

6 mint leaves, shredded

$^1/_4$ cup crème fraîche *or* sour cream

$3^1/_2$ oz smoked salmon slices

**2 teaspoons salmon roe, caviar, *or* lumpfish roe (or a
   combination of these)**

Peel potatoes if desired, then grate on a coarse grater. Mix with egg, onion, salt, and pepper. Halve mixture, roll into balls, and flatten between your hands into 2 disks about $^2/_3$ inch thick—you now have röstis. Heat a frying pan brushed with a little butter or oil. Add röstis and fry for a few minutes over moderate heat until golden. Turn and cook until golden on the other side.

  Mix mint into crème fraîche. To serve, place a rösti on a plate, lay some sliced salmon on top, then add a dollop of minted crème fraîche and a little mound of salmon roe.

Rosemary, potato, and feta flatbread

This is similar to a thick pizza. Add whatever toppings you want, but if they are too moist, they will prevent a crusty base from forming. Mashed kumara (or sweet potato) can replace the mashed potato for a richer taste.

Serves 6

1$^1/_3$ cups mashed potatoes, at room temperature (no salt added)

$^2/_3$ cup barely warm water

1 tablespoon dried yeast

about 3$^1/_3$ cups flour (bread or high grade)

1 cup polenta

2 teaspoons salt

1 large rosemary branch, leaves removed and finely chopped

2 red onions, finely sliced

6$^1/_2$ oz feta

$^1/_3$ cup extra virgin olive oil

Preheat oven to 500°F. Mix together mashed potatoes and water. Add yeast, stir well, and let stand for 20 minutes. Transfer into a large bowl and add half the flour, mix well, then add polenta, salt, and half the remaining flour.

Knead, working into a moist but manageable dough, adding more flour if necessary. Add half the rosemary, knead again, then cover the bowl with plastic wrap and leave in a warm place for 40 minutes.

Punch dough down and transfer to a lightly oiled baking sheet. Press or roll out to a $^1/_4$-inch thickness. Sprinkle with finely sliced red onion rings and remaining rosemary. Crumble feta on top, drizzle with half the oil, and let rise in a warm place for 20 minutes. Bake on the lowest shelf for 20 minutes or until base is crisp. Move to top of oven and cook for 10 minutes longer. Remove from oven and drizzle with remaining oil. Best eaten straight from the oven, but it makes a good picnic bread too.

Fava bean purée

You can make this from fresh or frozen beans. Just make sure you hull them to help keep the color greenish. Serve as a dip with slices of pita bread as you would hummus.

Serves 6 to 8 as a starter

1 medium-large white onion, peeled and thinly sliced

3 tablespoons extra virgin olive oil

2 cloves garlic, peeled and sliced

about 1 lb fava beans, cooked, refreshed, and hulled

1 large handful flat-leaf parsley

$^1/_3$ cup thick yogurt

juice of 1 lemon

salt and freshly ground black pepper

Sauté onion in half the oil until softened and barely golden. Add garlic and cook until soft. Allow to cool. Place beans in a food processor with parsley, add cooled onion mixture, and blend to a paste. Add yogurt, lemon juice, and remaining oil and blend again. Season to taste.

Salmon, dill, and mascarpone nori roll

Toasted nori is what usually comes wrapped around your sushi. Here it is teamed with European ingredients. Cut each roll in half for a picnic portion or into smaller pieces for canapés.

Makes 4

- ³/₄ cup (6¹/₂ oz) mascarpone *or* cream cheese
- ¹/₂ cup chopped dill
- 2 pinches salt
- ¹/₂ teaspoon cracked black pepper
- 4 sheets toasted nori
- 4 large, thin slices smoked salmon (about ¹/₂ lb in total)

Mix mascarpone with dill, salt, and pepper. Lay a sheet of nori on a cutting board and place a slice of salmon on top. Spread with a quarter of the mascarpone mixture, leaving a 1¹/₄-inch border at the end furthest from you. Roll up tightly. Use a pastry brush or your finger to seal the edge with a little cold water. Let rest for 20 minutes in the fridge to firm up, sitting on the seam, before cutting up with a very sharp knife.

Tofu, carrot, asparagus, and ginger spring roll

Tofu, a good source of protein, binds the other filling ingredients together in these delicious rolls.

Makes 8

- 1 medium onion, peeled and finely sliced
- 1¹/₂ tablespoons sesame oil
- 8 shiitake mushrooms, stems removed and finely sliced
- 1 carrot, peeled and julienned or grated
- 1 thumb fresh ginger, peeled and finely grated
- 8 oz tofu, crumbled
- 4 asparagus spears (ends snapped off and discarded), finely sliced
- pinch salt
- 8 (10-inch) square spring-roll wrappers
- 1 egg, beaten
- vegetable oil for deep frying

Fry onion in sesame oil until colored. Add mushrooms and carrot. Fry until carrot begins to soften. Remove from heat and mix in ginger, tofu, and asparagus. Season with a little salt.

Separate wrappers and lay them on top of each other in a diamond shape. Place one-eighth of filling in the center of wrapper, going from left to right, leaving 1¹/₂ inches on each side. Generously brush the point of the diamond furthest from you with beaten egg, then fold the point closest to you over filling.

Fold the two sides into the center, then roll the spring roll tightly away from you, using egg wash to hold the seams together. Make remaining spring rolls the same way. Deep-fry in hot oil (350°F) until crispy, then drain on paper towels. Serve with chile or peanut sauce.

Beef, avocado, bell pepper, and cucumber roll

This may seem an unlikely family of flavors, but it really does work for a hot summer's brunch.

Serves 2

**$^1/_2$-lb piece beef fillet (at room temperature), brushed with a
little oil**

1 long cucumber

1 roasted red bell pepper, peeled and seeded

$^1/_2$ avocado

grain mustard

pinch salt

Heat a skillet or frying pan over a high heat. Sear beef on all sides (about 6 minutes total cooking time). Let rest for 5 minutes.

Using a potato peeler, peel cucumber into wide strips. Cut bell pepper into strips as wide as the cucumber. Peel avocado, remove pit, and cut flesh into small wedges.

The next step is a little tricky. Place the fillet on a cutting board and, with a sharp knife, begin cutting a $^1/_2$-inch strip from the bottom, rolling the fillet as you go to make one long, thin strip. Then cut in half lengthwise. Lay two cucumber strips on the board and place half the beef on each one, spread some mustard on the beef, and sprinkle with a little salt. Lay some pepper on top, then roll up. Wrap some more cucumber around the roll to secure it, then poke pieces of avocado into the beef.

Roasting and peeling bell peppers

Many people find it difficult to remove the skins from peppers, so here are some pointers:

Grill or barbecue peppers until the skin blackens and blisters. Place in a bowl, covered with plastic wrap, and let cool. The blackened skin should now peel away easily.

If you have gas burners, you can sit the peppers directly on the flame and turn gradually until they blacken all over.

Alternatively, cut the peppers in half, remove stems, and press them flat with your palm against a cutting board. Turn on the broiler and place the peppers $^3/_4$ to $1^1/_2$ inches under the heat, skin side up, until skin blisters and blackens.

Yet another way is to cut the peppers into quarters, lay them cut side down in a roasting dish, and drizzle with a few tablespoons of oil. Seal the dish with foil, then place in a very hot oven for 15 to 30 minutes. The skins should easily come away.

Pumpkin and spinach tortilla

A tortilla is also known as a Spanish omelette, or in Italy you would call it a frittata, but don't confuse a Mexican tortilla with a Spanish one. The former is made with flour, and the latter, as in the following recipe, is made with eggs. Tortillas are best made at least six hours ahead and are even better eaten the day after you make them.

Serves 8 as a starter

$^3/_4$ cup extra virgin olive oil

3 onions, peeled and finely sliced

14 large eggs, lightly beaten

$^1/_4$ cup fresh oregano leaves

$1^1/_4$ lb roasted pumpkin or squash, cut into
  $^3/_4$-inch cubes

$^1/_2$ cup finely sliced green onions

$6^1/_2$ cups fresh spinach, blanched, water squeezed
  out, and chopped

$1^1/_2$ teaspoons sea salt

freshly ground black pepper

Heat a 12-inch deep-sided frying pan over a high heat. Add $^1/_4$ cup of the oil and, when it's hot, add onions, stir well, and cook until golden. Crack eggs into a bowl and add oregano, pumpkin, green onions, spinach, and cooked onions. Season with salt and pepper and mix well.

  Put the pan on full heat again and, when it is smoking, add remaining oil. Carefully pour omelette mix in and after 20 seconds stir gently. Bring the cooked outside into the center and take the raw center to the outside. Do this a few times, then turn heat down. You can now finish it either under the broiler or in the oven if you have an ovenproof pan (at 400°F) or on top of the stove (covered, on medium heat). It is cooked when just set—overcooked eggs are tough. Cool 10 minutes, then invert onto a large plate. Serve at room temperature.

Kumara, feta, and smoked paprika tortilla

Kumara is the native sweet potato I wrote about in the introduction—you can replace it with regular sweet potato. Keep this simple and serve with a salad and crusty bread.

Serves 6

$^2/_3$ lb kumara *or* sweet potatoes, peeled and cut into
  $^1/_2$-inch cubes

$^1/_3$ to $^1/_2$ lb potatoes, peeled and cut into $^1/_2$-inch
  cubes

2 teaspoons spicy smoked paprika

$^3/_4$ cup extra virgin olive oil

1 large red onion, peeled and finely sliced

3 tablespoons sherry vinegar *or* balsamic vinegar

10 large eggs, lightly beaten

1 cup feta, roughly crumbled

3 green onions, finely sliced

$1^1/_2$ teaspoons sea salt

freshly ground black pepper

Carrot, apricot, and pine nut fritters

I've based these fritters on ones I've had in Turkey, usually made with walnuts instead of the pinenuts—they're also delicious made with hazelnuts or pistachios. Kirmizi biber are delicious, slightly oily chile flakes from Turkey. If you can't get them, replace with regular chile flakes or finely chopped red chile. Serve these fritters hot or cold as a starter, with thick yogurt mixed with chile flakes and cilantro.

Serves 6 to 8 as a starter

1 lb carrots, peeled and halved

1 large handful parsley

2 tablespoons chopped dill

12 mint leaves

2 cloves garlic, peeled and chopped

1 teaspoon kirmizi biber *or* chile flakes

1 egg

1 cup fresh breadcrumbs

$^1/_3$ cup lightly toasted pine nuts, roughly chopped

8 dried apricots, finely chopped

1 level teaspoon salt

1 scant cup flour for dusting

oil for frying

Steam carrots until tender, then transfer to a colander to cool. Place in a food processor with parsley, dill, mint, garlic, kirmizi biber, and egg and purée to a paste. Place in a bowl and add breadcrumbs, pine nuts, apricots, and salt. Mix well. The mixture should be slightly sticky, but if it is excessively moist, add more breadcrumbs. Divide into about 20 pieces, then roll in flour and form into cylinders or patties. Refrigerate for half an hour.

Heat a little oil in a frying pan and cook fritters until golden on both sides, turning to prevent them from browning too much. Drain on paper towels.

Preheat oven to 400°F. Mix kumara and potatoes with paprika and half the oil. Lay on a roasting pan and bake until potatoes are just cooked. Meanwhile, fry onion in 2 tablespoons of the oil until caramelized. Add vinegar and cook until it evaporates. Crack eggs into a bowl and lightly whisk, then add onion and kumara mixtures, along with the oil they were cooked in. Add feta, green onions, salt, and pepper and mix well.

Heat a 9$^1/_2$-inch ovenproof frying pan, add remaining oil, and, when it begins to smoke (just a few seconds), add the egg mixture all at once. Let bubble for 10 seconds, then shake (or toss if you're feeling confident), bringing the cooked outer reaches into the center and the runny center to the outside. Do this a few times, then turn heat down and cook 1 minute.

Transfer to the top shelf of the oven and cook 8 to10 minutes. It's ready when the eggs are just set. Cool 5 minutes, then give the pan a gentle shake to loosen the tortilla, using a blunt knife to help if needed. Invert onto a plate. Cool before covering and storing in the fridge.

Corn and oyster fritters with sour cream and chives

I serve these as a nibble with a glass of champagne or a bellini (prosecco and peach-juice cocktail) when guests arrive. Serve two per person. If you're not an oyster fan, just omit them.

Makes 12

1 large egg plus 1 egg white

$^1/_3$ cup polenta

$^1/_2$ teaspoon salt

$^2/_3$ cup sour cream

$^3/_4$ cup corn kernels, fresh or canned
(see page 10)

2 green onions, sliced

12 oysters, out of the shell (drain off juice and wash and reserve shells)

butter *or* oil for frying

1 tablespoon finely sliced chives

Mix egg and white with polenta, salt, and half the sour cream. Stir in corn. Let stand 10 minutes. Mix in green onions and oysters.

Heat a little oil or butter in a frying pan and dollop in small spoonfuls of mixture, allowing one oyster per fritter. Cook until fritters begin to firm slightly, then flip and cook no more than 10 seconds—you don't want to overcook the oysters. Flip back over and place on a platter or in the oysters' own shells, which have been washed well and warmed slightly. Dollop remaining sour cream on top of each fritter, then sprinkle with the chives. Eat while still warm.

Spinach and parmesan fritters

These make a good brunch dish, served with poached eggs and bacon.

Makes 4 to 8

1/2 lb fresh spinach

4 eggs

2 tablespoons finely grated parmesan

4 green onions, green leaves only, finely sliced

1/2 teaspoon salt

olive oil for frying

Wash spinach well and drain. While still a little wet, cook in a saucepan over moderate heat until wilted. Drain and, when cool enough to handle, squeeze out excess water and roughly chop. Mix with eggs, parmesan, green onions, and salt. Heat a few teaspoons of oil in a large frying pan. Spoon in some of the mixture and cook over a moderate heat until colored, then gently flip over and cook until the fritter is just set.

Chickpea and feta fritters

These also make a great breakfast or brunch served with bacon and eggs—or serve with a salad as a starter. Smaller ones are good as a canapé with a dollop of pesto or tapenade, and they make good picnic food. I've used pre-cooked pulses to save time, but you could cook them from scratch if you want. The result will be a little better, but will take up to twelve hours more, once you've soaked and cooked the chickpeas.

Makes 6 to 8

1 1/2 (15-oz) cans chickpeas, rinsed and drained

1 large egg

1/2 scant cup thick yogurt

2 tablespoons tahini paste

1 teaspoon salt

1 teaspoon baking powder

2 tablespoons cornstarch

5 oz feta, cut into 1/4-inch cubes or roughly crumbled

4 green onions, finely sliced

oil *or* butter for frying

Place three-quarters of the chickpeas in a food processor with egg, yogurt, tahini, salt, baking powder, and cornstarch. Purée to a coarse paste. Place in a bowl and mix in remaining chickpeas, feta, and green onions. Stand for 15 minutes. Heat a little oil or butter in a frying pan and add spoonfuls of the mixture. Cook over a moderate heat until golden, then gently flip over and cook until just set. Remove to a plate. (These fritters are very soft and can break if flipped too soon, so handle them gently and only flip when almost set.)

Chicken livers on rosemary porridge fritters

Any poultry or finely sliced calves' liver works well with this delicious recipe; just adjust your cooking times accordingly. (I prefer liver to be just beyond medium rare.) The little fritters are quite dense, so make them as thin as you can. The large amount of pepper gives them a real bite. Tamarind paste can be replaced with balsamic vinegar, lemon juice, or pomegranate molasses.

Serves 6 as a starter

$1^1/_4$ cups quick oats

1 cup milk

$^1/_4$ cup ($^1/_2$ stick) butter plus $^1/_2$ cup (1 stick) extra
   for frying

1 teaspoon salt

1 teaspoon freshly ground black pepper (don't use
   finely ground pepper)

1 egg

2 green onions, finely sliced

$^1/_2$ teaspoon finely chopped fresh rosemary leaves

1 lb chicken livers, cleaned of all sinew

1 red onion, peeled and finely sliced

3 tablespoons tamarind paste

$^1/_2$ teaspoon ground star anise

$^3/_4$ cup boiling water

1 tablespoon soy sauce

1 small handful cilantro leaves

Place oats, milk, $^1/_4$ cup of the butter, and salt in a saucepan and slowly bring to a boil, stirring occasionally. Remove from heat and cool slightly. Mix in pepper, egg, green onions, and rosemary. Leave 20 minutes, then mix again. With wet hands, divide mixture into six balls and press flat. Heat a tablespoon of butter in a heavy frying pan. Fry until it stops sizzling, then add fritters. Cook on both sides until golden. Place on a warm plate and keep in a warm oven.

Add the remaining butter to the pan over high heat. When it begins to turn nut-brown, add livers and onion and fry until golden, about 30 seconds. Turn over quickly; add tamarind, star anise, and water; and bring to a boil. Simmer until cooking liquid is reduced to a thin syrup, add soy sauce and cilantro, and turn off heat.

To serve, place a fritter on each plate, spoon the livers on top, and then top with the sauce.

Asparagus with orange hollandaise and parmesan

This is the sort of thing you go out to eat at a café, but do try making it yourself—hollandaise sauce isn't as difficult as it seems. Practice and it will become a breeze.

Serves 4

1 teaspoon salt

20 to 32 asparagus stems (depending on size), ends snapped off and discarded

2 oz parmesan

few teaspoons snipped chives

Make hollandaise first and keep in a warm place (if it's too hot it may separate).

Bring a deep saucepan of salted water to a boil and add asparagus. Boil 1 to 2 minutes—the size of the asparagus will determine how long it needs. Drain well, then lay on a towel to soak up any remaining moisture. Divide between four plates, spoon on hollandaise, shave on some parmesan, and sprinkle with chives.

Orange hollandaise

1 cup (2 sticks) butter

2 eggs plus 1 extra yolk

2 teaspoons finely grated orange zest

2 tablespoons orange juice

salt and freshly ground black pepper to taste

Melt butter in a small saucepan; then move to the side of the stove to keep warm—the butter should not be hot. Take a deep saucepan about $9^1/_2$ inches in diameter and fill with $1^1/_2$ inches of hot water. Heat to a gentle boil.

Place eggs, yolk, zest, and juice in a metal bowl about 12 inches in diameter. Whisk well; then place on top of the saucepan. Beat with a whisk or egg beater until mixture thickens, about 3 to 4 minutes. Take bowl off the heat, set on a damp towel to keep it from sliding around; and trickle in melted butter, whisking continually. Season.

Prawn cocktail

This strangely likeable entrée has earned a warm welcome back into kitchens in the last few years. Here's my version of a classic. Great served with crunchy toast. Nashi is also known as Asian pear—if you can't find one, replace with a good crunchy pear.

Serves 4

2 medium-sized, ripe avocados, peeled and pits removed

1 nashi, cored but unpeeled

2 tablespoons chopped parsley

2 tablespoons extra virgin olive oil

1 tablespoon lime juice *or* lemon juice

salt and freshly ground black pepper

$2/3$ lb cooked prawns *or* shrimp, shells removed

about $1/4$ cup mayonnaise

Cut avocados and nashi into $1/4$-inch cubes and mix with parsley, oil, and juice. Season with salt and pepper. Place a round cookie cutter or metal ring in the center of a plate and gently press a quarter of the mixture inside to make a flat disk. Run a knife around the inside of the cutter and lift it up. Do the same on three more plates. Divide the prawns into four and set a pile on each disk. Dollop some mayonnaise on top.

Battered mussels with Tarator sauce

The two most common ways you'll see mussels served in Istanbul are stuffed in the shell with rice or served just like this. Tarator is one of Turkey's great sauces, sometimes made with hazelnuts, pistachios, or pine nuts. Ideally, you should use mussels that haven't been cooked, just shelled like you would an oyster. But you can use cooked mussels if necessary.

Serves 6 to 8 as a starter

$1^1/3$ cups flour

1 teaspoon kirmizi biber *or* chile flakes

1 teaspoon salt

3 teaspoons sugar

1 teaspoon baking powder

1 cup beer, at room temperature

oil for deep frying

30 to 40 fresh mussels, shelled

extra flour for dusting mussels

Sift flour, kirmizi biber, salt, sugar, and baking powder into a bowl. Slowly whisk in beer, making sure there are no lumps. Stand 10 minutes. Heat cooking oil in a deep saucepan. Lightly dust mussels with a little flour, then dip them into the batter. Carefully drop into hot oil, one by one, and cook until the batter is golden (it may be best to cook them in several batches). Drain on paper towels. Serve with the sauce and a lemon wedge.

Edna's grilled sardines on toast

This is a tasty dish that takes no time to make. My partner, Michael, serves it cut into fat strips with a soft-boiled egg—perfect. His mother, Edna, used to make it for him as a little boy in London's Thornton Heath. It's important to use good-quality sardines, ideally preserved in olive oil.

Serves 2

10¹/₂ oz canned sardines

1 tablespoon plus 1 teaspoon balsamic vinegar

4 slices best white bread (sourdough is great)

2 tablespoons extra virgin olive oil

salt and freshly ground black pepper to taste

Mash sardines, the oil they come in, and half the vinegar with a fork. Toast bread on both sides. Brush one side with half the oil and spread with sardines. Broil until beginning to bubble. Drizzle with remaining oil and vinegar and broil until golden. Season. Eat very hot.

Tarator sauce

Ideally made in a mortar and pestle, you'll probably make this sauce in a food processor at home. The walnuts must be the best quality—older ones can become rancid, ruining the taste of the sauce.

2 thick slices 1-day-old bread

¹/₂ cup walnuts, lightly toasted

3 cloves garlic, peeled

3 tablespoons lemon juice

5 tablespoons extra virgin olive oil

salt and freshly ground white pepper

Lightly toast bread, then soak in water for 1 minute. Squeeze out water and place in a food processor with walnuts and garlic. Purée to a coarse paste, then pulse in lemon juice and slowly drizzle in olive oil. Place in a bowl and season well.

Chorizo, kumara, and kumquat chutney burger

I came up with a chorizo and sweet-potato burger for GBK, a New Zealand—owned burger company based in London, and it's proven very popular. Here is a different version, but it's the same principle of spice and sweetness that makes it work so well.

Serves 2

1 smallish orange kumara *or* sweet potato, about $^1/_3$ to $^1/_2$ lb

salt and freshly ground black pepper

3 chorizo sausages, about $^1/_2$ to $^2/_3$ lb

2 ciabatta rolls, oven warmed

extra virgin olive oil

3 tablespoons Kumquat and Pear Chutney (recipe on page 31)

1 handful arugula leaves

Slice kumara into $^1/_4$-inch-thick slices and steam or boil until just cooked. Season well and put aside.

Halve chorizo lengthwise or cut into $^1/_2$-inch rings. Heat a frying pan or barbecue and brown chorizo for 1 minute on both sides, taking care that they don't burn. Split rolls and drizzle both halves with a little olive oil. Spread a little chutney on the bottom halves. Lay kumara on top, then arugula, chorizo, a good dollop of chutney, and finally the lids.

Spicy roast beef and hummus in pita bread

The first "meal" I made in home economics at Wanganui High School was an open sandwich—hardly inspiring, but here I am twenty-seven years later giving a recipe for a sandwich. Pitas are a great lunch staple because you can fill and wrap them easily.

Serves 2

- 3 tablespoons hummus
- 1 tablespoon tahini
- 1 tablespoon mayonnaise
- $^1/_3$ lb roast beef, thinly sliced and cut into strips
- 2 pita breads
- 1 handful salad leaves
- 2 tablespoons cottage cheese
- $^1/_4$ red bell pepper, thinly sliced
- 1 tablespoon chile sauce
- mustard cress to garnish

In a small bowl, mix the hummus, tahini, and mayonnaise, then mix in the beef. Halve pita breads or cut a slit $^1/_2$ inch from the top. Gently pry them open and push in some salad leaves. Spoon half the beef mixture into each one, top with cottage cheese and bell pepper, spoon on some chile sauce, and garnish with cress.

Home-cured beef fillet with cucumber and ginger pickle

Cure the beef for this entrée in advance as it will keep for up to two weeks. And don't be put off by this recipe's long method—the effort is well worth it.

Serves 6

- 2$^1/_4$ cups (1 lb) brown sugar
- about 1 lb coarse sea salt
- 2 tablespoons malt vinegar
- 14 oz center-cut beef fillet
- 1 small thumb fresh ginger, peeled
- $^1/_2$ cucumber
- 1 tablespoon superfine sugar
- 6 ($^1/_2$-inch-thick) slices sourdough bread
- 1 clove garlic, peeled
- extra virgin olive oil for drizzling

Begin curing beef at least 4 days before you want to serve it. Put two layers of 18 x 12 inch plastic wrap on a work surface. Mix sugar, salt, and vinegar together in a bowl and add beef. Rub salt mixture into beef, then lay lengthwise on the plastic wrap.

Spread all of the salt mixture over beef and roll it up tightly, expelling any air. Ideally, the beef should be evenly covered with salt mixture. Wrap some more plastic wrap around it, place in a container, and refrigerate. For the next three days, turn beef over 180 degrees every 12 hours.

Once cured, remove beef from plastic wrap and gently rinse under cold water to remove any excess salt mixture. Pat dry with a towel and refrigerate, covered, for up to two weeks.

The day before you want to serve, finely grate ginger and coarsely grate cucumber, skin and all. Place ginger and cucumber in a bowl with the sugar. Mix well, then cover and refrigerate overnight.

Just before serving, squeeze liquid from cucumber. Toast bread and rub one side of each slice with raw garlic, then drizzle with a little olive oil. Finely slice beef and lay it on the bread, then dollop some cucumber mixture on top.

Melon, mint, and honey smoothie

This is quick to make and tasty. For an Indian lassi drink, add half a cup of plain, thick yogurt.

Serves 2

$^1/_2$ to $^3/_4$ medium-sized green melon, diced (discard skin and seeds)

1 small handful mint leaves

1 tablespoon light honey

$^1/_4$ cup lime juice

15 ice cubes

Place everything in a blender and purée well. Add extra honey if needed.

Melon and kiwi lassi

This great breakfast drink contains all you'll need to start the day with a zing. Any variety of melon will work, although cantaloupe is my favorite.

Serves 2

$^1/_2$ to $^3/_4$ medium-sized melon, peeled and seeded

2 kiwi, peeled and halved

$^3/_4$ cup plain thick yogurt, chilled

2 to 4 tablespoons manuka honey *or* other rich honey

6 large ice cubes

Place all ingredients in a blender and blend for 20 seconds. Add more honey if desired.

Berry and pineapple punch

Fruity and very simple. Although this recipes calls for Lemon & Paeroa (L&P), a favorite childhood drink from the town of Paeroa in New Zealand's North Island, you can replace it with any lemon-flavored lemonade. It can also be blended together to make a delicious smoothie. If you can't get hold of fresh red currants and raspberries, then by all means use frozen.

Serves 6 to 8

$1^2/_3$ oz hulled red currants *or* cranberries

$3^1/_2$ oz raspberries

$3^1/_2$ oz hulled strawberries, halved

$^1/_4$ cup plus 1 tablespoon superfine sugar

$^1/_2$ scant cup white rum *or* vodka (optional)

3 large handfuls ice cubes

$2^1/_2$ cups pineapple juice

$2^1/_2$ cups Lemon & Paeroa

Crush all the currants and half the berries in a bowl with the sugar, then mix with the remaining berries. Mix in rum or vodka, ice, and pineapple juice and pour into a jug, then stir in the L&P.

sauces, salsas, and relishes

Here are some nice tangy chutneys and relishes, exciting salad dressings, pickles, and a few fruity accompaniments. These recipes can turn the ordinary into the exciting. Imagine serving your friends a poached chicken with salad. Now imagine also placing on the table a jar of pickled red plums and a dish of spicy black bean and peanut salsa. You'll be justified in looking a little smug, and your friends will welcome the delicious treats.

Roast nectarine chutney

Roast nectarine chutney

This delicious chutney, made in the oven and thereby not necessitating continual stirring in a saucepan, can be made with any stone fruit, but I personally love it made from almost overripe nectarines. This will give you a bit more than two 1-pint jars, depending on the size of your nectarines.

15 nectarines, pitted and quartered

4 cloves garlic, roughly chopped

6 red onions, peeled and finely sliced

1 lemon, halved, then finely sliced and seeded

2 tablespoons rosemary leaves

1 bouquet garni

1 teaspoon cumin seeds

1 teaspoon fennel seeds

1 cup cider vinegar

$2^1/_2$ cups demerara *or* raw sugar

3 teaspoons Thai fish sauce

Preheat oven to 400°F. Put all ingredients except sugar and Thai fish sauce into a large ceramic roasting dish. Mix well, then place on upper shelf of oven and roast 45 minutes, stirring occasionally. Once the mixture begins to reduce and color, add sugar and Thai fish sauce and cook for 30 minutes more, stirring twice during this period. The chutney should be thick and the fruit still discernible in shape. (Continue cooking if it is too moist.)

Fill sterilized glass jars with hot water to prime, then wipe dry and add chutney. Leave just $^1/_4$ inch at top of each jar. Seal while still hot and let cool. Store in the fridge for at least one week before eating. Once opened, make sure you keep it refrigerated.

Kumquat and pear chutney

Kumquats are a really beautiful, if not cute, fruit. They are not always easy to get hold of, so you can replace them with orange, lemon, or mandarin. This chutney goes well with cheese or cured meats—or use it to finish the Chorizo, Kumara, and Kumquat Chutney Burger (page 24).

Makes about $2^1/_2$ cups

$^1/_3$ lb kumquats *or* 1 orange, lemon, *or* mandarin, finely diced

$1^1/_4$ cups superfine sugar

3 tablespoons water

1 large red onion, peeled and finely sliced

3 pears, skin on, cored, and diced

$^3/_4$ cup cider vinegar

2 teaspoons salt

$^1/_2$ cinnamon stick

4 cardamom pods

$^1/_2$ teaspoon chile flakes

2 whole cloves

1 teaspoon ground allspice

Halve kumquats and remove seeds. Place sugar and water in a saucepan and set over a low heat until sugar dissolves. Turn up heat and bring to a boil. Cook over a high heat without stirring until it caramelizes (turns golden brown).

Add kumquats and red onion and stir to break up the toffee that will form as the cold ingredients hit the hot caramel. Add remaining ingredients and bring to a boil, then turn the heat down to medium and cook with a lid on for 30 minutes, stirring occasionally to stop it sticking to the bottom.

Remove lid and cook until liquid has reduced by at least half and the chutney has thickened (30 to 40 minutes). Pour into hot, clean jars, then seal and cool before storing in the fridge for at least a week before using.

Pickled plums

These are a mainstay of my menus. I serve them with any-thing from roast duck breast to curried chicken. Choose firm plums that are just ripe. You can use the leftover pick-ling liquid as part of a salad dressing, with some extra vir-gin olive oil added. These are what I call "fridge pickles," as you need to keep them in the fridge all the time.

Makes 2 1-quart jars

  2 cups cider vinegar

  1 quart (4 cups) water

  2^1/$_2$ cups demerara *or* raw sugar

  2 cinnamon sticks

  ^{1}/$_4$ cup finely grated fresh ginger

  2 cloves garlic, peeled

  6 star anise

  2 bay leaves

  2 allspice

  3^1/$_2$ tablespoons best soy sauce

  2^1/$_4$ lb plums, halved and pitted

Bring all ingredients except plums to a boil and simmer uncovered for 15 minutes. Fill 2 quart preserving jars with hot water, then drain and pack in the plum halves. Pour boiling pickling liquid over (adding any of the pieces from the saucepan) while it's still hot, then seal and cool completely. Refrigerate for at least a week to pickle before eating.

Creamed coconut relish

This is great with a spicy curry—the creaminess and sweet-ness work well to temper lots of spice.

Serves 8

  3 cups shredded coconut

  2 tablespoons mustard seeds (black or yellow)

  2 tablespoons currants *or* cranberries

  ^{2}/$_3$ scant cup apple juice

  1 cup crème fraîche

  ^{1}/$_2$ scant cup thick yogurt

  1 large lemon, finely grated zest and juice

  1 smallish bunch cilantro leaves, chopped

  1 teaspoon salt

Preheat oven to 350°F. Place coconut and mustard seeds on a baking tray and bake until coconut is golden, about 5 minutes. (Cooked too little it will taste indiffer-ent, but cooked too much it will taste bitter and burned.) Meanwhile, place currants and apple juice in a small saucepan, cover, and bring to a simmer. Cook 5 minutes, remove lid, and cook until liquid has evaporated. Trans-fer to a bowl and cool in the fridge.

   Once cold, blend crème fraîche, yogurt, and lemon juice and zest in a bowl. Mix in coconut, currants, cilantro, and salt. Let rest 30 minutes before serving.

Coconut, cucumber, and yogurt relish

This goes well with curries from all over the world—it's the sharpness of the yogurt mixed with the fresh crunch of the cucumber that does it.

Serves 8

1 cup shredded coconut, lightly toasted

$^1/_2$ long cucumber, halved, seeded, and coarsely grated

$^3/_4$ cup thick, plain yogurt

1 clove garlic, peeled and crushed

$^1/_2$ cup tightly packed cilantro leaves, roughly chopped

$^1/_2$ cup tightly packed mint leaves, finely shredded

$^1/_2$ teaspoon salt

$^1/_2$ teaspoon hot mustard paste (English mustard)

juice of 1 lime *or* lemon

Mix all ingredients together and let it sit in the fridge for at least 1 hour before serving.

Raw apple, date, and walnut relish

This keeps in the fridge for a day or so, or, if simmered for a few minutes, it will keep for a few days. It goes really well with cold cuts or spread in sandwiches with cheese.

Serves 6

1 medium red onion, peeled and finely diced

$^1/_2$ red chile, seeded and finely chopped

3 tablespoons freshly squeezed orange juice

about 1 cup walnuts, roughly chopped

3 tablespoons olive oil

2 Granny Smith apples, cores removed

10 fresh or dried dates

Mix onion and chile with orange juice and let it marinate for 1 hour. Gently fry walnuts in oil until just beginning to turn golden. Remove from heat. Grate apples and combine with onion mixture. Remove pits from dates, chop finely, and add to the apple mixture with walnuts and oil. Mix well and taste for seasoning.

Spiced strawberry and ginger jam

This jam is a personal favorite. It's great on cheddar cheese scones, spread thinly over cold smoked ham, or on whole-meal toast with goat cheese. Strawberries have a low level of pectin (the soluble carbohydrate that makes jam set), so you may want to add a pectin-based setting agent as extra insurance when you make this. These are available from supermarkets and come with instructions.

Makes 2¹/₃ pints

- 3 lb strawberries, rinsed and hulled
- 3 lb superfine sugar
- ¹/₃ lb ginger, finely julienned
- 2 red chiles, finely chopped (include seeds)
- ¹/₂ lemon, sliced into 4 pieces and seeded
- 3 teaspoons ground allspice

Mix strawberries and sugar in a large bowl, cover with plastic wrap, and refrigerate for 24 hours. Place in a saucepan and slowly bring to a boil with ginger, chiles, lemon, and allspice. Boil 5 minutes, stirring well. Place back in the bowl and leave 48 hours in a cool place.

Boil for another 20 minutes, stirring well. Check that jam has set by placing a little on a saucer and allowing it to cool. Push your finger across the top—if the surface wrinkles, the jam is ready. Pour into sterilized jars, seal immediately, and refrigerate for 1 week before using.

Rosemary, garlic, and chile glaze

This glaze is something I like to drizzle over roast or grilled meats. It may seem odd to add something sweet to cooked meats, but chutneys work well with meat, and you may find this another good accompaniment. It goes particularly well with richer or fattier meats such as pork, lamb, venison, or chicken.

For 10 chops

- ³/₄ cup superfine sugar
- 3 tablespoons water
- 3 tablespoons rosemary leaves, roughly chopped
- 8 cloves garlic, peeled and finely sliced
- 1 small red chile, finely sliced (remove seeds for a milder version)
- ¹/₃ cup balsamic vinegar
- 3 tablespoons water
- ¹/₂ teaspoon salt
- 1 teaspoon freshly ground black pepper

Place sugar and water in a small saucepan and bring to a boil, stirring until dissolved. Once it comes to a boil, don't stir. When it becomes a caramel color (about 7 minutes), add rosemary, garlic, and chile and gently stir. The caramel will burn if you're not careful. After 10 seconds, add vinegar, water, and seasonings and simmer for another 2 minutes.

Rosemary, garlic, and chile glaze

Fruity barbecue sauce

This is sweet, spicy, aromatic, and tangy—all that a barbecue sauce should be. Smother it over barbecued meats and fish. Leftover sauce can be kept in the fridge for a day or two (as long as you haven't dipped meat in it). Remove chile seeds for a milder sauce.

Serves 8 to 10

- 1 ripe mango, peeled and pit removed
- 3 ripe tomatoes, quartered
- 2 red chiles, stems removed
- 1 medium onion, peeled and quartered
- 2/3 cup malt vinegar
- 1/4 cup tomato paste
- 1 teaspoon ground cloves
- 1 teaspoon cumin seeds
- 1 cup firmly packed brown sugar

Place mango, tomatoes, chiles, onion, and vinegar in a blender or food processor and pulse to a smooth paste. Add tomato paste and spices and purée 10 seconds. Pour into a saucepan and bring to a boil. Stir in sugar and simmer until thickened.

Red currant and cherry relish

This can be made up to a week in advance and kept in the fridge. In the Southern Hemisphere this makes a great relish to serve alongside the Christmas turkey or ham, as the summer cherries will be out.

Serves 6 to 8

- 1 cup superfine sugar
- 3 tablespoons orange juice
- zest of 2 oranges, finely julienned
- 10 1/2 oz red currants, off the stem, *or* cranberries
- 10 1/2 oz pitted cherries
- 2/3 cup red wine vinegar
- 1 red chile, finely chopped
- 1 clove garlic, finely chopped
- 1 bay leaf

Place sugar and juice in a pan and bring to a boil; stir until sugar dissolves. Cook over a high heat until sugar caramelizes, then add zest and fruit. Stir well and cook for 2 minutes. Add vinegar, chile, garlic, and bay leaf and rapidly simmer 5 minutes, until the sauce thickens. Pour into a sterilized jar and tightly seal. Keep refrigerated.

Spicy roasted apricots

I like to serve stone fruit cooked like this with almost any roast—except perhaps beef. This is quick to make and adds a special twist to the menu. It can be made up to two days in advance.

Serves 6

9 to 12 apricots, halved and pits removed

1 fresh red chile, finely chopped

1 small thumb fresh ginger, peeled and grated

2 star anise

2 cloves

1 teaspoon coriander seeds

4 tablespoons sugar

$^1/_3$ cup cider vinegar

$^1/_2$ teaspoon salt

Preheat oven to 400°F. Lay apricots in a nonmetal roasting dish. Place everything else in a saucepan and bring to a boil. Boil 20 seconds, then pour over the apricots. Bake until some of the fruit begins to color (about 15 to 20 minutes). Serve hot or cold.

Nashi and kiwi salsa

I once served a variation of this salsa as a canapé topping at a function in the shadow of the Windsor Castle for New Zealand's national rugby team, the All Blacks. Unfortunately, they didn't win their next game—but I hardly think I'm to blame! At home, I have served it on grilled salmon, then used the leftovers the next day on a ham sandwich. If you can't find a nashi (or asian pear), use a good, sweet crisp pear instead.

Serves 4 as an accompaniment

1 nashi, cored and diced

3 kiwi, peeled and diced

1 medium red onion, peeled and finely sliced

6 chives, finely sliced

1 lime, finely grated zest and juice

6 basil leaves, finely sliced

3 tablespoons extra virgin olive oil

1/2 teaspoon salt

few good grinds black pepper

Mix all the ingredients together and check seasoning. Leave salsa to steep for 1 hour before using, mixing again just before serving.

Spicy black bean and peanut salsa

The black beans to use here are not Chinese salted black beans. They are, in fact, a dried bean usually associated with Mexican or Spanish cooking. This salsa is delicious eaten with grilled corn on the cob, grilled fish, and grilled meats.

Serves 6 to 8

3/4 cup dried black beans *or* black-eyed beans

1 red onion, peeled and finely diced

2 tablespoons cooking oil *or* peanut oil

4 cloves garlic, peeled and finely chopped

1 to 2 hot green chiles, finely chopped

1/2 cup roasted peanuts, roughly chopped

2 tablespoons finely grated dark chocolate

1/2 teaspoon finely ground cinnamon

1/4 teaspoon finely ground cloves

1 small bunch cilantro, leaves picked and stems chopped

Place beans in a saucepan and cover with plenty of cold water (so that you have 4 inches of water above the beans); place a lid on the pan and bring to a boil. Cook 1 minute, then turn off heat and let beans sit for 1 hour.

Drain beans and again cover with plenty of cold water, bring to the boil, stir well, and simmer until just cooked. The cooking time will vary depending on the type and freshness of beans. Drain beans and briefly rinse with cold water.

Fry onion in oil until golden brown. Add garlic and chiles and stir. Remove from heat and mix in peanuts and chocolate, then mix in beans, spices, and cilantro.

Check seasoning and serve at room temperature. This will keep in the fridge for 1 day.

Spicy black bean and peanut salsa

Melon, feta, and pine nut salsa

Okay, okay, I admit it—this is based on one of my favorite salads, which appeared in my Sugar Club Cookbook. But I often make this version to use as a salsa on crostini, grilled fish, and chicken. And it's a good way to use up leftover wedges of melon.

Serves 8 to 10 as an accompaniment

1 smallish melon *or* 2 different-colored halves,
   peeled, seeded, and diced

5 oz feta, cut into same-sized cubes

$2/3$ cup pine nuts, toasted

3 tablespoons extra virgin olive oil

juice of 1 lime *or* $1/2$ lemon

2 green onions, finely sliced

freshly ground black pepper

pinch salt

Combine all ingredients and leave for 20 minutes. Mix again, then serve.

Chunky chorizo, tomato, and kumara salsa

This is more like a stew than a salsa. It makes a delicious base on which to set chunks of grilled fish, lamb chops, or grilled duck breasts. You could also replace the water with three times the amount of vegetable stock to make a delicious thick soup. It is a good dish to help boost other flavors, rather than being a dish in itself.

1 tablespoon olive oil

1 large red onion, peeled and diced

1/3 to 1/2 lb chorizo, peeled and cut into 1/2-inch
   cubes

3 cloves garlic, peeled and finely chopped

1/2 thumb fresh ginger, chopped

1 1/4 lb kumara *or* sweet potatoes, scrubbed and cut
   into 1/2-inch cubes

2 large tomatoes, cut into 1/2-inch cubes

3/4 cup water

1/2 teaspoon dried (or fresh) oregano

1/2 teaspoon sweet smoked paprika

2 green onions, sliced

Heat oil in a saucepan and cook onion over a moderate-high heat until it begins to caramelize. Add chorizo, garlic, and ginger and cook 1 to 2 minutes to release the fat from the chorizo. Add remaining ingredients except green onions and bring to a boil. Stir, cover, and simmer until kumara is just cooked, 8 to 10 minutes. Remove lid, gently stir again, and cook 4 to 5 minutes to reduce liquid. Just before serving, stir in green onions.

Citrus, sesame, chile, and peanut dressing

This dressing goes well with many proteins—chicken, tuna, salmon, pork, and tofu. All benefit from the sweet and sour taste and crunchy texture. A mixture of orange, grapefruit, lime, and lemon juices can be used, or you may want to use just one. This is best made on the day you want to use it, as the nuts lose their crunch if left too long.

Makes 8 to 10 servings

1 cup superfine sugar

2 tablespoons water

1/2 cup lightly toasted skinless peanuts, roughly
   chopped

1 chile, finely chopped

1 clove garlic, peeled and finely sliced

2 teaspoons toasted sesame seeds

1 cup citrus juice

1/2 scant cup soy sauce

1/2 scant cup peanut oil

Place sugar and water in a saucepan and bring to a boil, stirring to dissolve the sugar. Remove the spoon and cook on a high heat until the sugar caramelizes. (Be careful not to burn.)

Add peanuts, chile, garlic, and sesame seeds and stir over a moderate heat for 15 seconds. Add citrus juice and boil 1 minute. Remove from heat and add soy sauce and peanut oil. Serve at room temperature.

Tomato, thyme, lemon, and fennel seed dressing

This incredibly simple dressing is a good way to get tomatoes on the dinner table—without having to see red! It is also a good way to use up slightly overripe or broken-skinned tomatoes. It goes well with white meats, fish, or salads.

Serves 10 to 15

1 lb ripe tomatoes, cut into quarters

1 clove garlic, peeled

2 large teaspoons fresh thyme leaves

2 ripe lemons, finely grated zest and juice

1 teaspoon fennel seeds, toasted

1 1/4 cups extra virgin olive oil

1/2 teaspoon salt

1/2 teaspoon freshly ground black pepper

Place everything in a blender and purée for 30 seconds, check seasoning, then purée for a further 10 seconds. That's it!

Peach, ginger, and chile dressing

This goes really well with grilled or barbecued meats, especially pork chops. It keeps in the fridge for a day or two.

Serves 6

3 ripe peaches, skin on and pits removed

1 small thumb fresh ginger, peeled and sliced,
   or 1 piece candied ginger

1 to 2 red chiles, sliced

2 cloves garlic, peeled

juice of 1 large lemon

8 large mint leaves

3/4 cup salad oil

1 teaspoon salt

Place all ingredients in a blender and purée to a fine consistency. You may want to pass the dressing through a fine sieve if you don't like the texture of the peach skin.

Aïoli

In its most basic form, this is a garlic mayonnaise. It is great used in the same way you would use plain mayonnaise. I always make mine with saffron, as it adds an earthy flavor. It is important to make aïoli with light oil, not extra virgin olive oil, as this will become bitter. It will keep in the fridge for seven days if kept tightly covered. You can make this using a mortar and pestle, a whisk and round-bottomed bowl, or a small food processor.

Makes about 1 1/2 cups

10 saffron threads

2 1/2 tablespoons fresh lemon juice

1 large egg plus 1 extra yolk

4 cloves garlic, peeled and chopped

1/2 tablespoon English mustard

1/2 teaspoon salt

1/2 teaspoon freshly ground black pepper

1 1/4 cups salad *or* light olive oil

2 teaspoons hot water

Soak saffron in lemon juice for 15 minutes, then put mixture in a small food processor with egg and yolk, garlic, mustard, salt, and pepper. Purée for 30 seconds, scraping down the bowl halfway through. Slowly drizzle oil in while the motor is running. When you have added half the oil, turn the machine off and scrape down the sides of the bowl, then turn machine back on and continue to add the remaining oil. Lastly, add hot water (this helps stabilize it).

Salad dressings

Just whisk all ingredients together. All these recipes make enough for four to six salads.

Lebanese dressing

1/4 cup pomegranate molasses

1/2 scant cup olive oil

1 teaspoon tahini

1/2 teaspoon salt

Japanese dressing

2 tablespoons finely chopped pickled ginger

2 tablespoons mirin

2 tablespoons rice vinegar

1/2 scant cup sunflower oil

1 tablespoon miso paste

Italian dressing

1 clove garlic, peeled and crushed

2 tablespoons balsamic vinegar

1/2 cup extra virgin olive oil

1/2 teaspoon salt

Chinese dressing

1 tablespoon hoisin sauce

1 teaspoon sesame oil

2 tablespoons black *or* malt vinegar

1/2 cup sunflower oil

Thai dressing

4 limes, zest and juice

1/2 red chile, seeded and finely chopped

2 teaspoons Thai fish sauce

1 tablespoon grated palm sugar *or* brown sugar

1/2 cup peanut oil

1 teaspoon roasted crushed peanuts

soups

Soups are really satisfying things to make, and they're versatile: they can be served cold in summer or hot in winter, there's a soup for every occasion, and they can be served as a starter or a main course. I've often served the broth from a meaty stew as a first course and the "chunky bits" as the main course. Soups can be made using very few ingredients, and even leftovers are a good source of inspiration. My rule of thumb tends to be to sauté onions or leeks, add herbs and spices, then often add something starchy such as pulses, rice, or root vegetables. Add stock and simmer until cooked. Then purée it or leave it chunky. Soup often improves with a day or two's aging in the fridge, much like a stew, so it doesn't always have to be a last-minute job. Just remember when reheating it to use a heavy-bottomed pan and stir frequently over a low to moderate heat, so as not to burn the bottom.

Kumara, lentil, and cumin soup with balsamic onions

Rich and earthy, this makes a hearty winter meal with lots of crusty bread.

Serves 4 to 6

- $^1/_3$ cup (5$^1/_3$ tablespoons) butter
- 1 large onion, finely diced
- 1 teaspoon cumin seeds
- 12 sage leaves, torn in half
- 1 medium leek, washed and finely sliced
- 2 cloves garlic, peeled and sliced
- 1 large orange kumara *or* sweet potato, about 1 pound, peeled and cut into $^1/_2$-inch cubes
- $^1/_4$ cup split red lentils, rinsed
- 1 quart (4 cups) vegetable stock *or* water
- 3 tablespoons olive oil
- 1 large red onion, finely sliced
- 3 tablespoons balsamic vinegar
- 1 large handful chopped parsley

Melt butter in a deep saucepan over a high heat until nut-brown and foamy. Add onion and cumin seeds. Cook 2 to 3 minutes, stirring to prevent burning. Add sage, leek, garlic, and kumara and stir well. Add lentils and stock and bring to a boil. Simmer 30 minutes or until lentils and kumara are tender.

While soup is cooking, heat oil in a small frying pan, add red onion, and cook over a moderate heat, stirring occasionally, until it begins to caramelize. Add vinegar, cook until it has evaporated, then remove from heat.

Adjust soup for seasoning and stir in parsley. Ladle into bowls and dollop the onions on top.

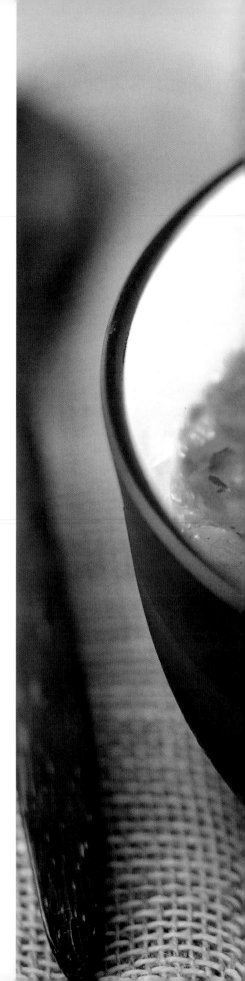

Parsnip, rutabaga, and almond soup with sesame snails

This chunky soup is an intriguing combination of delicious flavors.

Serves 6 to 8

$1^1/_2$ tablespoons butter

2 tablespoons olive oil

2 teaspoons sesame oil

1 large leek, washed and finely sliced

1 tablespoon fresh rosemary leaves

$3/_4$ cup blanched almonds, coarsely
chopped

$1/_2$ to 1 lb parsnips (about 2 medium),
peeled and cut into chunks

$1/_2$ lb rutabaga (about $1/_2$ medium),
peeled and cut into chunks

$1^1/_2$ teaspoons sweet smoked paprika

$3^1/_3$ cups vegetable stock

$1^1/_4$ cups cream *or* crème fraîche

4 tablespoons tahini

1 sheet thawed puff pastry

2 tablespoons sesame seeds

few tablespoons sliced chives

Heat butter and oils in a deep saucepan and then sauté leek, rosemary, and almonds until leek wilts and almonds are golden. Add parsnips and rutabaga, paprika, and stock and bring to a boil. Cover and simmer 45 minutes or until vegetables are tender. Add cream and half the tahini and bring back to a boil. Check seasoning.

While the soup is simmering, spread remaining tahini over pastry and sprinkle with sesame seeds. Roll up tightly to form a long roll and wrap in plastic. Freeze 30 minutes. Cut into $1/_2$-inch slices and lay on a lined baking sheet, giving them plenty of room to expand. Bake at 450°F for 8 to 10 minutes. Ladle soup into bowls, garnish with chives, and serve with a warm sesame snail.

Andalusian-inspired gazpacho

This may seem like a nongenuine version, as you may be used to a chunky gazpacho, but, believe me, this is what it's like if you go to Andalusia. Summer is the best time to enjoy this easy, refreshing soup—tomatoes and peppers are plentiful and at their most flavorsome then.

Serves 6 as a starter

1¹/₄ lb ripe tomatoes, quartered

2 large red bell peppers, seeds and stems removed

1 clove garlic, peeled

2 tablespoons lemon juice

¹/₄ cup dry sherry

2 slices stale white bread, crusts removed, cut into
   ³/₄-inch cubes

1³/₄ cups cold water

¹/₄ cup extra virgin olive oil

1 teaspoon sea salt

2 hard-boiled eggs, peeled and roughly chopped

2 green onions, finely sliced

Place all ingredients except egg and green onions in a blender and purée well for 1 minute, then strain through a sieve into a large bowl. (It may be easier to do this in two batches.) Season with extra salt to taste. Serve chilled, poured over ice cubes, and garnished with egg and green onions.

Zucchini, pine nut, parmesan, and mint soup

This is a distant cousin of a soup I created for an Air New Zealand menu on flights from London to Los Angeles a few years back.

Serves 4 as a starter

1 large onion, peeled and finely diced

2 tablespoons extra virgin olive oil

$^1/_4$ cup finely chopped pine nuts

2 cups coarsely grated zucchini

$2^1/_2$ cups vegetable stock

$^3/_4$ heaping cup finely grated parmesan

$^1/_4$ cup finely sliced mint leaves

$^1/_4$ cup sour cream (optional)

Fry onion in olive oil over a moderate heat until it has caramelized. Add pine nuts and fry until they take on color. Add zucchini and cook, stirring occasionally, for another 2 minutes.

Add stock and bring to a boil, then turn to a simmer and cook 5 minutes. Stir in parmesan and mint. Check seasoning. Serve with a dollop of sour cream on top.

Kumara, porcini, and red lentil soup with cheddar

I devised this soup recently when faced with one of those "I wonder what's in the cupboard" meals. Not everyone has a packet of dried porcini in their cupboard, but if you do buy some, remember they keep for up to twelve months in an airtight jar away from sunlight.

Serves 4

1 onion, peeled and sliced

1 teaspoon fresh rosemary, finely chopped

4 cloves garlic, peeled and sliced

2 tablespoons extra virgin olive oil

1 large kumara *or* sweet potato, about 1 lb, peeled and diced

6 cups vegetable stock *or* water

$^1/_2$ cup dried red lentils

$^1/_4$ cup dried porcini

$^3/_4$ heaping cup grated cheddar *or* parmesan *or* pecorino

Fry onion, rosemary, and garlic in olive oil until golden, then add kumara. Fry 1 minute and add stock. Bring to a boil and add lentils and porcini. Bring back to the boil and stir to prevent lentils sticking to the bottom. Cover and simmer until kumara is tender. Check seasoning. To serve, ladle into bowls and scatter the cheese on generously.

Spinach, watercress, and mint soup with lamb dumplings

This soup can be served as a starter or in larger portions as a main course for two. Chunks of roasted pumpkin and left-over cooked rice can be added to make it more substantial.

Serves 4

- 3 tablespoons extra virgin olive oil
- 2 medium leeks, washed and finely sliced
- 1 small onion, finely diced
- 2 cloves garlic, peeled and finely sliced
- 1 bay leaf
- 1 bunch watercress, washed and finely chopped
- $3^1/3$ cups vegetable stock
- $1/3$ to $1/2$ lb ground lamb
- 1 cup loosely packed mint leaves, chopped
- 1 tablespoon cornstarch
- $1/2$ teaspoon salt
- 2 shallots, peeled and finely diced
- 5 cups fresh spinach leaves, washed and roughly chopped

Heat oil in a deep saucepan and add leeks, onion, garlic, and bay leaf. Sauté gently for 5 minutes, stirring occasionally. Add watercress and stir well. Add stock and bring to the boil, then turn to a simmer.

Mix lamb with half the mint, all the cornstarch, salt, and diced shallots. Mix well and roll into marble-sized balls. Add to soup and poach for 5 minutes. Stir in spinach and remaining mint, check seasoning, and bring to a boil. As soon as it comes to a boil, take it off the heat and serve.

Scallop and potato soup

This soup is more like a broth, with a fresh, light taste. You can also make it with any flaky fish—just poach the fish in the broth, remove and flake the flesh, and return it to the soup.

Serves 4

- 1 medium leek, well washed and finely sliced
- 1 lb potatoes, peeled and cut into $1/2$-inch cubes
- 3 tablespoons extra virgin olive oil
- 1 stem lemon grass
- $1/3$ hot red chile, finely sliced
- 3 cups fish stock *or* vegetable stock
- $1^1/2$ tablespoons Thai fish sauce
- 8 large scallops, seasoned and lightly brushed with oil
- $1/4$ cup cilantro leaves

Fry leek and potatoes in olive oil in a large saucepan until the leek begins to color. Cut the bottom $3/4$ inch of the stem from the lemon grass and peel off the outer two layers; discard these (or save in the freezer to use in a stock later). Finely slice the lower half of the remaining lemon grass stem and add this to the pan with the chile and the unsliced upper half—you'll have to discard this upper half when you serve the soup. Add fish stock and bring to a boil, then add Thai fish sauce and simmer until potato is cooked.

Meanwhile, heat up a heavy frying pan and add scallops. Cook 30 seconds on each side. Remove pan from heat and let cool.

Once potatoes are cooked, taste broth for seasoning, adding extra salt if needed. Slice each scallop into four pieces horizontally and add them to the broth to warm through for 10 seconds. Remove from heat and serve in deep bowls garnished with a little cilantro.

Chilled melon, ginger, kumara, and yogurt soup

Any ripe aromatic melon will work well with this, except watermelon, which is too watery. Make the soup a day ahead if you can so the flavors become more rounded. If you think it needs thinning, just mix in some melon or apple juice.

Serves 6

2 tablespoons light olive oil

1 large kumara *or* sweet potato, about 1 lb, peeled and diced

1 medium leek, sliced and washed well

1/2 red chile, sliced

1 to 2 thumbs fresh ginger, peeled and finely sliced

1³/4 cups water

1 teaspoon fresh thyme

1 scant teaspoon salt

1 medium-large ripe melon, seeded, peeled, and roughly chopped

1³/4 cups thick yogurt, plus a little extra for garnish

salt and freshly ground black pepper

chives for garnish

Heat a heavy saucepan and add oil, kumara, and leek. Cover and fry over a moderate heat, stirring occasionally. Once kumara begins to color, add chile and ginger and continue to cook, covered, until kumara is tender.

Add water, thyme, and salt and rapidly simmer, covered, for 10 minutes. Remove from heat and cool for 20 minutes. Purée soup to a fine texture, adding melon at the same time. Cool completely, then whisk in yogurt and refrigerate overnight. The next day, season to taste.

To serve, ladle soup into chilled bowls, add a teaspoon of yogurt, and sprinkle some chives on top.

Garlic, chorizo, and chickpea broth with egg noodles

The gutsy flavor of chorizo makes this a wonderfully flavorsome soup. This is another of those "almost-a-meal-in-itself" soups.

Serves 6 to 8

12 cloves garlic, peeled and halved

$1/3$ cup extra virgin olive oil

$1/3$ to $1/2$ lb chorizo sausage

2 large red onions, diced

1 tablespoon rosemary leaves, roughly chopped

1 tablespoon fresh oregano leaves, roughly chopped

$1 1/2$ (15-oz) cans chickpeas, drained and rinsed

2 bay leaves

1 lemon, finely grated zest and juice

4 cups chicken *or* vegetable stock

1 egg

2 teaspoons cold water

2 pinches salt

1 teaspoon olive oil

Cook garlic in oil in a very small frying pan over a gentle heat, stirring occasionally, until soft and golden, about 20 minutes. Remove with a slotted spoon. Peel any casing from chorizo and slice half into thin discs. Fry disks in the same oil that you cooked the garlic in, until cooked. Remove with a slotted spoon and set aside. Cut remaining chorizo into small cubes.

Transfer oil to a deep saucepan. Add onions, diced chorizo, rosemary, and oregano and fry until they begin to caramelize. Add caramelized garlic, chickpeas, bay leaves, lemon zest, and stock and bring to a boil. Simmer 30 minutes.

Beat together egg, water, and salt. Heat a 6-inch nonstick frying pan and brush with 1 teaspoon oil. Drizzle in egg mixture so it covers base of the pan. Cook over a moderate heat until just set. Transfer to a cutting board, roll up, and cut the egg into $1/2$-inch slices. Unroll into "noodles."

Taste broth for seasoning and stir in lemon juice. Ladle into bowls and serve with egg "noodles" and chorizo disks on top.

Pumpkin, coconut, and lemon grass soup with cod

A truly delicious mixture of textures and flavors. Sort of Southeast Asian in origin but served with a meaty white fish—here I use New Zealand's delicious blue cod. You can use any fish that is at its best at the time.

Serves 6 as a hearty starter

3 tablespoons light cooking oil

2 large onions, peeled and sliced

2 cloves garlic, peeled and sliced

1¹/₄ lb peeled pumpkin, diced

2 lemon grass stems

¹/₄ teaspoon saffron *or* **¹/₂ teaspoon turmeric**

2 tablespoons tamarind paste *or* **pomegranate molasses**

1³/₄ cups unsweetened coconut milk

3 cups water

2 tablespoons Thai fish sauce

²/₃ lb cod fillet, skinned and cut into thick slices

2 tablespoons cornstarch

1 teaspoon salt

3 tablespoons butter

freshly ground black pepper

Heat oil in a deep saucepan. Add onions and garlic and cook until wilted but not colored. Add pumpkin, lemon grass (use only the bottom 3 inches: cut off the base, remove the outer two layers and discard, then finely slice the inside), saffron, tamarind paste, coconut milk, water, and Thai fish sauce and bring to a boil. Cover and simmer 40 minutes. Purée in a blender—you may need to do this in batches. Return to pot and bring back to a simmer and check seasoning.

Place cod, cornstarch, and salt in a small plastic bag and shake to coat fish. Heat butter in a frying pan. When it turns brown, add fish pieces and fry for 30 seconds each side or until cooked through.

To serve, ladle soup into shallow bowls and place fish pieces on top. Grind on some black pepper.

Tomato, ginger, and carrot soup with croutons

This soup pays homage to my childhood, but with a twist. This is quite a thick soup, which can be thinned with tomato juice or vegetable/chicken stock if desired.

Serves 4 to 6

$^1/_4$ cup olive oil

2 medium red onions, finely sliced

2 cloves garlic, peeled and chopped

1 large carrot, peeled and finely grated

1 bay leaf

1 thumb fresh ginger, peeled and finely grated

1 (28-oz) can peeled tomatoes, chopped

$1^1/_2$ tablespoons butter *or* a few tablespoons olive oil

4 slices white bread

salt and freshly ground black pepper

2 green onions, finely sliced

Heat oil in a deep saucepan. Add onions and cook over a moderate to high heat, stirring occasionally, until beginning to caramelize. Add garlic, carrot, bay leaf, and ginger and sauté 3 to 4 minutes. Add tomatoes and bring to the boil. Cover and simmer gently for 15 minutes.

To make croutons, butter or oil bread and cut into $^3/_4$-inch squares. Cook under a broiler until golden on both sides.

To serve, check soup for seasoning, adding salt and pepper to taste. Ladle into bowls, scatter croutons on top, and sprinkle with green onions.

Savoy cabbage, bacon, parsnip, kumara, and chickpea soup

In the depths of winter, a hearty soup can be a meal in one bowl. Jean Cazals, the photographer who makes these dishes I cook look so good, said it was lovely—what more can I say!

Serves 6

2 medium leeks, washed and finely sliced

2 parsnips, peeled and cut into $^3/_4$-inch cubes

6 rashers bacon, rind off, cut into $^1/_4$-inch pieces

7 tablespoons butter

$^1/_2$ small savoy cabbage, core removed and finely shredded

10 sage leaves

1 teaspoon fresh thyme

1 small kumara *or* sweet potato, skin scrubbed and cut into $^1/_2$-inch cubes

1 small can (15 oz) chickpeas, drained and rinsed

4 cups vegetable *or* chicken stock

salt and freshly ground black pepper

Fry leeks, parsnips, and bacon in butter over a moderate heat until leeks begin to take on a little color. Add cabbage, herbs, kumara, and chickpeas and mix well, then add stock and bring to a boil. Turn to a simmer and cook until kumara and parsnip are tender. Check seasoning; add a little salt and pepper if desired.

Savoy cabbage, bacon, parsnip, kumara, and chickpea soup

Bean, spinach, corn, and chicken laksa

Laksa is a soup that you'll find in restaurants and food stalls in Malaysia and Singapore, consisting of a chile-fired broth, noodles, and sprigs of cilantro and often served with crispy shallots sprinkled on top. Add more of anything you want to this laksa—treat it as a melting pot for your favorite flavors. Don't worry if fresh baby corn is unavailable, as the dish is still delicious without it.

Serves 4

2 small onions, finely sliced

1 leek, washed and finely sliced

2 green chiles, finely sliced

$1^1/_2$ tablespoons sesame oil

2 cloves garlic, peeled and crushed

2 to 3 tablespoons finely grated ginger

2 star anise

4 kaffir lime leaves

2 lemon grass stems

$3^3/_4$ cups light chicken stock

2 teaspoons Thai fish sauce

2 chicken breasts, cut in half lengthwise and lightly brushed with sesame oil

8 fresh baby corn, brushed with a little sesame oil (if using canned, rinse and pay dry)

20 green beans, trimmed

3 cups fresh spinach, coarsely shredded

3 tablespoons lime juice

$2^1/_2$ oz rice vermicelli noodles, cooked and rinsed

$^1/_2$ small bunch cilantro

12 mint leaves

Preheat oven to 400°F. Sauté onions, leek, and chiles in sesame oil until onions start to caramelize, stirring well. Add garlic, ginger, star anise, lime leaves, and lemon grass (remove the two outer layers and finely slice $1^1/_2$ inches of the thickest part; discard the rest) and fry for another minute. Add chicken stock and Thai fish sauce, bring to a boil, then turn to a gentle simmer.

In a frying pan, brown chicken on all sides, add the corn, toss it a little, then transfer to a baking pan and roast in oven until just cooked, about 12 minutes. Remove from the oven and finely slice the chicken when it's cool enough to handle.

Bring "stock" back to the boil and add green beans, boil 1 minute, then add corn and chicken. Return to the boil and stir in spinach and lime juice, check seasoning, and remove from heat. Divide vermicelli between four warmed bowls and then pour laksa over them. Top with cilantro and mint leaves.

Roasted pumpkin, garlic, and rosemary soup with pepitas and feta

The fleshy New Zealand pumpkins, which I miss so much in England, are perfect for this delicious soup. This is one of those soups that almost tastes better reheated the next day. Pepitas are pumpkin seeds, by the way.

Serves 6 to 8

1 lb pumpkin, peeled, seeded, and cut into $3/4$-inch chunks

12 cloves garlic, peeled and halved

2 large onions, peeled and sliced

$3/4$ cup pumpkin seeds, lightly toasted

2 tablespoons fresh rosemary leaves, roughly chopped

$1/2$ scant cup extra virgin olive oil

$3^{1}/3$ cups vegetable stock

$3^{1}/2$ oz feta

Preheat oven to 350°F. Line a roasting dish with baking paper. Mix the pumpkin, garlic, onions, pumpkin seeds, rosemary, and olive oil together and place in the dish. Bake, stirring every 10 minutes, until pumpkin is cooked and golden (about 45 minutes). Place in a food processor and blend to a chunky paste. Bring the stock to a boil and add the paste. Stir well and bring to a simmer, adding more stock if required. Check seasoning and simmer 5 minutes. Serve with feta crumbled on top.

salads

Salads are in many ways as versatile as soups. They can be as simple as arugula drizzled with lemon juice and olive oil or as complex as something like a salad Niçoise. Dressings (see Sauces, Salsas, and Relishes chapter) are as important in a salad as the ingredients themselves. Here's where an excellent extra virgin olive oil and a good vinegar come to the fore. You won't need to use excessive amounts—they may cost quite a bit, but they do last. Remember to use the olive oil within a year of purchase, as it will deteriorate over time, and keep it in a cool place away from light. Most salads benefit from being tossed together at the last minute, especially those with green leaves, as dressings tend to make the leaves wilt.

Melon, nut, green bean, and parmesan salad

Numerous flavors and textures, from crunchy through to smooth and crisp, make this salad surprisingly complex.

Serves 6

1 medium-sized, sweet honeydew melon

1 large handful (1/4 lb) green beans, trimmed, blanched, and rinsed to cool

1 cup mixed nuts, lightly toasted

2 oz parmesan, finely grated

2 tablespoons lemon juice

5 tablespoons olive oil *or* salad oil

salt and freshly ground black pepper

Peel melon, remove and discard seeds, then cut into 3/4-inch cubes. Place in a salad bowl with beans, nuts, and half the parmesan. Mix lemon juice and oil with a few pinches of salt and a few grinds of black pepper.

Pour over the salad and mix well. Just before serving, sprinkle on the remaining parmesan.

Thai beef salad with lime dressing

Thai beef salad must be one of the new classics of the last twenty years. It appears all over the place and owes its success to the combination of sweet and sour with crunchy textures and fresh herby tastes. I like to add rice, as it provides yet another layer of flavor to the dish, but it is optional. Remember to serve this as soon as you make it. It is also great made with chicken, duck, or salmon instead of beef.

Serves 6 as a starter

1 lb beef fillet, trimmed, cut horizontally into two equal thin pieces

oil for frying

2 teaspoons uncooked rice, dry roasted in the oven (or slowly cooked in a small frying pan over moderate heat) until golden-brown, then finely ground in a spice grinder (optional)

4 shallots, peeled and finely sliced

The Providores slaw

Named after our London restaurant, we first served this slaw at an outside dinner in Cowes on the Isle of Wight in honor of Team New Zealand to promote the America's Cup, that much-prized yachting trophy. Jicama is the South American name for what the Chinese call "yam bean," so head to either an Asian or a South American market if you can't find it in your local grocery store.

This version serves 12, although we made enough for 200!

$1/2$ small green *or* red cabbage

1 green papaya *or* mango, peeled and seeded

1 large kohlrabi, peeled

$1/2$ jicama, peeled, *or* 2 nashi (asian pears)

$1/2$ cucumber, seeded

1 red onion, peeled

$1/2$ scant cup lemon juice

2 teaspoons finely grated lemon zest

1 scant cup extra virgin olive oil

2 teaspoons salt

1 teaspoon freshly ground black pepper

2 teaspoons manuka honey *or* other rich honey

1 cup flat-leaf parsley leaves

Finely slice or julienne (on a mandolin) all the vegetables and the papaya and place in a large bowl. Whisk together remaining ingredients, except parsley, and pour over vegetables. Toss well and chill 30 minutes. Mix in parsley.

1 cup picked cilantro leaves

$1/2$ cup picked mint leaves from the tips

$1/2$ cup peanuts, toasted and coarsely chopped

Sear beef strips in a very hot frying pan with a little oil, being careful to cook no more than rare. Allow beef to rest for 10 minutes in a warm place.

Slice the beef thin and place in a mixing bowl; add lime dressing, roasted rice, shallots, herbs, and peanuts; and mix well. Divide into six even mounds and serve immediately.

Lime dressing

6 limes

2 teaspoons palm sugar *or* raw sugar

$1/2$ red chile, finely chopped (remove seeds for a milder taste)

$1/2$ teaspoon Thai fish sauce

$1/2$ teaspoon tamari (wheat-free soy sauce)

Finely grate zest from 3 limes and then juice all of them. Mix this with sugar, chile, Thai fish sauce, and tamari until the sugar is dissolved.

Kumara, parmesan, and basil salad

The sharpness of the parmesan complements the sweetness of the kumara in this salad. Try this with grilled poussin breast or pan-fried salmon fillet or a white fish that you've marinated in a little lime juice and ginger. Or serve it as a starter with a good helping of arugula or watercress.

Serves 6 as a starter

- 2 lb kumara *or* sweet potatoes, peeled and cut into $3/4$-inch chunks
- $1/2$ scant cup olive oil
- 5 oz parmesan, coarsely grated or peeled into shards
- 1 cup loosely packed basil leaves (tear the larger ones into quarters)
- $1/3$ cup lime *or* lemon juice
- $1/2$ scant cup olive oil

Preheat oven to 400°F. Toss kumara with 2 tablespoons of the olive oil and season lightly, then lay on a baking tray and roast until cooked. Cool, then cut into $1/2$-inch cubes and toss with the remaining ingredients. Allow to stand for 10 minutes before serving.

Potato, chorizo, green bean, and bell pepper salad

The true pleasure of this salad comes from its combination of texture, flavor, and color. Sherry vinegar can be replaced with balsamic or a good red wine vinegar.

Serves 4 as a starter

- $2/3$ lb spicy chorizo, removed from casings and cut into $1/4$-inch slices
- 2 tablespoons olive oil
- 1 lb new potatoes, boiled and halved
- $1/2$ teaspoon salt
- $2 1/3$ cups (about $2/3$ lb) green beans, blanched
- 3 red bell peppers, grilled or roasted, skin removed, then sliced
- 2 tablespoons sherry vinegar

Fry chorizo in batches in a little oil, removing to a plate once done. (Chorizo should be as crisp as possible.) Add potatoes and salt to the frying pan and fry for 1 minute or until slightly browned. Transfer to a bowl, scraping any crunchy bits in as well. Add beans, bell peppers, remaining oil, and sherry vinegar. Toss well. Scatter chorizo on top.

Potato, chorizo, green bean, and bell pepper salad

Carrot, cardamom, and mint salad

Try this with grilled squid, mackerel, or white fish or with a large dollop of hummus in warmed pita bread.

Serves 6 as a starter

$^2/_3$ scant cup cider vinegar

$1^2/_3$ cups water

1 cardamom seed pod, crushed

$^1/_3$ cup sugar

1 teaspoon salt

2 cloves garlic, peeled and thinly sliced

4 medium carrots

$1^1/_2$ tablespoons extra virgin olive oil

$^1/_4$ cup chopped fresh mint

$^1/_4$ cup chopped parsley

Bring vinegar, water, cardamom, sugar, salt, and garlic to the boil in a saucepan and simmer rapidly for 5 minutes. Meanwhile, peel and trim carrots. Using a potato peeler, peel ribbons from carrots. Add carrots and olive oil to the pan and stir to mix it all together, then place a lid on and bring to a boil. Cook 1 minute, then remove from heat, stir again, and allow to cool in pan. Just before serving, stir in chopped mint and parsley.

New potato and pea salad with mint dressing

This dish has a wonderfully fresh taste. It can be served on its own as a starter or as an accompaniment to chicken, poached fish, or cold roast leg of lamb. It's important to use small potatoes—if they're big, just cut them up.

Serves 4 as a starter

$1^1/_4$ lb scrubbed new potatoes

1 cup freshly hulled peas

1 leek, washed and finely sliced into rings

Put potatoes into a deep saucepan and cover with plenty of cold salted water and boil. When they're almost cooked, add peas and leek to the pot, bring back to a boil, and cook another 4 minutes. Test a pea— if it's ready, pour all of the contents into a colander and run cold water over them for a minute.

While vegetables are still warm, toss with dressing and let cool.

This salad can be made the day before, but you will find the peas lose their vivid color. To avoid this, cook them separately and mix in an hour or so before you serve the dish.

Marinated grapes with goat cheese

Fellow New Zealander Felicity Morgan-Rhind, a former chef and now a fabulous Auckland-based filmmaker, gave me this recipe. It is a real taste treat.

Serves 4 as a starter

1 red onion, peeled and finely sliced

3 tablespoons red wine vinegar

salt and freshly ground black pepper to taste

2 large handfuls sweet green grapes, halved and seeded (if you can be bothered)

3 tablespoons extra virgin olive oil

plenty of chopped fresh parsley and mint

6^1/$_2$ oz ripe goat cheese, chopped into ^{1}/$_2$-inch chunks

Place red onion and vinegar in a bowl and mix well. Season with a little salt and pepper and let stand for 20 minutes. Add halved grapes and olive oil, mix well, and marinate in the fridge for an hour.

Half an hour before serving, toss in the herbs and goat cheese. Serve this at room temperature.

Mint dressing

^{3}/$_4$ cup vegetable salad oil

^{1}/$_4$ cup extra virgin olive oil

1 cup firmly packed mint leaves

^{1}/$_3$ cup freshly squeezed lemon juice

1 tablespoon English mustard

2 teaspoons superfine sugar

^{1}/$_2$ teaspoon sea salt

freshly ground black pepper

The easiest way to make dressing is to place oils and mint into a blender or small food processor and blend for 30 seconds, then add all other ingredients and blend for another 10 seconds. Alternatively, finely shred mint and mix it with oils. Combine lemon juice and mustard, then mix everything together.

Warm green bean, egg, and potato salad with parmesan dressing

Warm green bean, egg, and potato salad with parmesan dressing

This is a lovely autumn or cool summer salad served with some toasted white bread to mop up the juices.

Serves 4 as a starter

1 lb small new potatoes, scrubbed

1 cup (about 1/4 lb) green beans, trimmed

1/2 scant cup olive oil

2 tablespoons balsamic vinegar

salt and freshly ground black pepper

1 small handful flat-leaf parsley

4 eggs, soft boiled, peeled and quartered

1²/₃ oz (about 1/3 cup) parmesan, freshly grated

Boil potatoes in plenty of salted water until just cooked. Add beans to the saucepan and boil another 2 minutes. Drain into a colander.

In a large bowl, mix oil and vinegar together, then add a little salt and a few grinds of pepper. Add potatoes and beans to dressing and mix well. Add parsley and mix again.

To serve, divide the salad between four plates and place the egg quarters on top. Eat while still a little warm. Serve the parmesan separately and sprinkle on at the last minute.

Red onion, cumin, and pine nut couscous salad

This is based on a recipe I learned over ten years ago from a Roman chef friend named Carla. It's best served at room temperature as part of a buffet-style lunch. It can be made up to 6 hours before serving.

Serves 4 to 6

2 cups instant couscous

1¹/₂ cups tepid water

1 teaspoon salt

1/2 teaspoon freshly ground black pepper

2 medium red onions, peeled and finely sliced

2 teaspoons fresh rosemary leaves

1/2 teaspoon cumin seeds *or* ground cumin (optional)

1/3 cup olive oil

²/₃ cup pine nuts, toasted

1/3 cup balsamic *or* sherry vinegar

4 green onions, finely sliced

Place couscous in a bowl and pour in water. Stir in salt and pepper.

Fry onions, rosemary, and cumin in oil until caramelized, stirring frequently. Add pine nuts and vinegar and cook over a high heat, stirring, until vinegar has almost evaporated. Pour mixture on top of couscous and mix in. Let stand 10 minutes, then add green onions, mix again, and serve.

Puy lentil, red onion, and yogurt salad

This is a lovely first course because it is dense, small, and complex in flavor. Serve it with warm flatbread. Sumac is a red berry from the Middle East. It is usually sold ground and has a pleasant astringent taste. If you can't find it, don't worry, as the dish will still taste great without it.

Serves 4 to 6 as a starter

 1 large red onion, peeled

 $^1/_4$ cup olive oil

 1 clove garlic, peeled and finely chopped

 1 teaspoon fresh ginger, grated or chopped

 $^1/_2$ cup puy *or* green lentils, rinsed under cold water and drained

 4 teaspoons soy sauce

 4 teaspoons vinegar

 2 tablespoons pomegranate molasses *or* tamarind paste

 $^1/_2$ scant cup thick yogurt

 1 large teaspoon sumac (optional)

Finely dice half the onion and fry in half the oil until it begins to caramelize. Add garlic and ginger and cook a little more, stirring well. Add lentils, soy sauce, and enough water to cover by $^1/_2$ inch. Bring to a boil and put a lid on. Cover and simmer 20 minutes, then check to see how they're doing.

If lentils are still chewy and there's no water in the saucepan, add a little extra hot water and cook until al dente. Remove lid and simmer until liquid has almost evaporated. Transfer to a bowl and let cool.

Heat remaining oil in a small frying pan and add the other half of the onion, finely sliced. Cook over a moderate heat until caramelized. Add vinegar and cook to evaporate it, then add pomegranate molasses and bring to the boil. Transfer into another bowl to cool.

To serve, spoon a small mound of lentils onto a plate, dollop on some yogurt, and sprinkle over a little sumac, then finish with a small pile of onions.

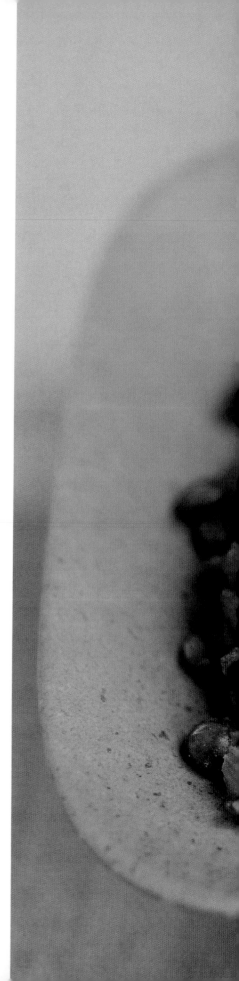

vegetables

Vegetables are the saving grace of cookery. Without them a meal would simply be a mass of protein. Much as I could happily munch away solely on a roast suckling pig and no veggies, as Michael and I did at Restaurant Botin in Madrid over Easter 2003 (which incidentally is recorded as the oldest restaurant in the world), what we craved when we left was something that once grew in or above the soil, that was born from a seed—a little steamed broccoli, grilled zucchini, or even a salad leaf! These recipes include stand-alone vegetarian dishes, side orders, and buffet-type dishes. If vegetables are cooked properly and with good seasoning and spicing, it is possible for them alone to satisfy die-hard carnivores.

Baked peppers stuffed with tomato, garlic, and basil

This recipe is based on that wonderful classic "Peppers Provençale," although normally they have anchovies in them. I've left them out, but if you want to be correct just add one salted anchovy fillet, rinsed and bones removed, to each pepper. These can be eaten as a first course or as part of a main course, but always at room temperature.

Serves 4

6 large tomatoes

1/2 scant cup extra virgin olive oil

4 large red bell peppers, halved and seeded

24 basil leaves

1 clove garlic, finely sliced

4 green onions, finely sliced

salt and freshly ground black pepper

Preheat oven to 400°F and heat a ceramic roasting dish (or roasting pan lined with baking paper). Peel tomatoes by bringing a saucepan of water to the boil. Score a cross in tomato skins without cutting too deep into the flesh. Place tomatoes in boiling water, not overcrowding the pan, and count to 20. Remove tomatoes and place in a bowl of cold water. Leave for a minute, then peel skin off with your fingers; it should come away easily, but if it doesn't, return to the pan for 10 seconds. Cut tomatoes into quarters.

Put a few teaspoons of olive oil into the preheated roasting dish. Cut peppers in half, remove seeds, and lay them cut side up in the dish. Divide basil, garlic, and green onions between peppers, then place three tomato quarters into each one, packing them in tight. Drizzle remaining oil over stuffed peppers and sprinkle with salt and pepper.

Bake 25 minutes until tomatoes have softened and peppers have taken on some color. Remove from the oven and let cool and mature for a few hours before eating or store in the fridge for the following day, when they'll taste just as good.

Peppers with goat cheese, chorizo, and olives

Bell peppers simply scream out to be stuffed—their shape was designed for it. These are great made the morning you plan to eat them and are best served at room temperature.

Makes 6

3 red bell peppers, halved and seeded

6^1/$_2$ oz goat cheese, cut into 12 slices

2 tablespoons olive oil

^{2}/$_3$ lb spicy chorizo sausage, cut into ^{1}/$_4$-inch-thick
   slices

2 cloves garlic, peeled and finely sliced

1^1/$_2$ cups assorted olives, pitted

1^2/$_3$ oz parmesan, grated (about ^{1}/$_3$ cup)

Heat oven to 350°F. Place peppers in a roasting dish lined with parchment paper. Place a slice of cheese in each one. Heat a frying pan and add oil and chorizo. Cook over a moderate heat until chorizo is colored. Add garlic and olives. Fry 1 minute, tossing occasionally. Spoon into peppers, lay another slice of cheese on top, and scatter parmesan over. Bake 15 minutes or until parmesan is golden brown.

Wok-fried brussels sprouts with chile, ginger, and garlic

Even people who, like me, don't really like brussels sprouts will be asking for seconds after trying this recipe. It's best to cook the sprouts in two batches to help keep them crisp. Chopped, roasted peanuts, basil, or cilantro can also be added for a really tasty dish.

Serves 6 as a side dish

^{3}/$_4$ to 1 lb brussels sprouts

2 tablespoons cooking oil (peanut oil is good)

1 hot red chile, finely sliced

1 thumb fresh ginger, finely grated or julienned

2 cloves garlic, peeled and finely sliced

1 teaspoon superfine sugar

2 teaspoons Thai fish sauce

^{1}/$_4$ cup hot water

Remove and discard any really thick leaves from brussels sprouts, then cut leaves from the base with a small knife, snapping them off as you go. If this seems too tedious, finely slice sprouts instead. Heat a wok over high heat and add half the oil. Once it's smoking, add half the sprout leaves and fry, tossing well, for 30 seconds. Add half of each measure of the chile, ginger, and garlic and toss well, then tip into a bowl. Wipe the wok, heat it up, and add the remaining oil. Once it's smoking, add the remaining sprouts, cook over a high heat for 30 seconds, tossing as you go, then add the remaining chile, ginger, and garlic. Return the first batch of sprouts to the wok, then add sugar and fry for another 40 seconds, caramelizing the sugar a little as you go. Add Thai fish sauce and water, toss well, and cook another minute. Serve at once.

Mushrooms braised with sake and ginger

I served these at home recently with some poached smoked haddock, a poached egg, and hollandaise—it was delicious. However, they're also good to serve alongside roast chicken or lamb. Some people prefer to peel their mushrooms, but I don't bother.

Serves 4 to 6

> 12 flat mushrooms
> 1/2 scant cup sake
> 1/2 cup (1 stick) plus 3 tablespoons butter
> 1 teaspoon fresh ginger, finely chopped
> 1 tablespoon soy sauce
> pinch salt
> freshly ground black pepper

Preheat oven to 350°F. Place mushrooms in a baking dish that has a lid. (Don't worry if they are a little squashed, as they will shrink as they cook.) Place remaining ingredients into a saucepan and bring to a simmer, then pour over mushrooms. Cover and bake 40 minutes.

Roast squash with peanut and garlic salad

I made this for the photo using a delicious new breed of squash grown in New Zealand called kuri squash, but butternut or small dark-skinned pumpkin works equally well. On balmy autumn days this can be served at room temperature, but on chilly days it is best served straight from the oven.

Serves 8 as a starter

- 2 small squash *or* 2 lb pumpkin *or* butternut cut into 16 wedges, seeds removed
- 16 cloves garlic, unpeeled
- 2 teaspoons sea salt
- $1/2$ scant cup extra virgin olive oil
- $1/2$ cup boiling water (from the kettle)
- $1/2$ cup lime juice (about 5 big, juicy limes)
- 1 teaspoon finely grated lime zest
- 1 red chile, finely chopped
- 2 teaspoons Thai fish sauce
- 2 teaspoons grated palm sugar *or* raw sugar
- $1^1/2$ cups peanuts, roasted and roughly chopped
- 1 cup cilantro leaves
- 1 handful mustard cress

Preheat oven to 400°F. Place squash in a ceramic or foil-lined baking dish. Scatter over garlic, salt, and oil. Pour in water. Roast 30 minutes or until squash is tender and garlic soft.

To make the dressing, mix lime juice and zest with chile, Thai fish sauce, and sugar until sugar dissolves.

To serve, place two wedges per person on a plate with 2 garlic cloves. Scatter over peanuts, cilantro, and cress. Spoon on dressing.

Barbecued corn with cilantro butter

I have become addicted to corn cooked like this, so in summer it's a regulation barbecue dish—and at work we char-grill the corn for the same effect. If neither are available, cook it in a hot, heavy frying pan.

Serves 4

4 corn cobs, husks removed

$1/2$ cup (1 stick) plus 3 tablespoons butter

1 cup roughly chopped cilantro leaves

1 small red onion, finely diced

salt and freshly ground black pepper

Rub oil over the corn, then place on a rack about 4 inches above the coals. Cook, turning regularly, until golden brown. Meanwhile, place butter in a small pan on barbecue and heat until it turns nut-brown. Stir in cilantro, remove from heat, then stir in onion. Keep warm. Spoon over cooked corn, sprinkle with salt and pepper, and eat before it goes cold.

Braised artichokes with lemon, thyme, and olives

I'm sure the reason a lot of people steer clear of artichokes is the "How do I prepare them?" worry. The truth, though, is that they are relatively easy to prepare with a little practice. The easiest thing to do is boil them whole and pull them apart as you eat them. But, for your guests, the method opposite is a more "user-friendly" way.

Serves 4 as a starter

1 cup good olive oil

1 large onion, peeled and thickly sliced

1 carrot, peeled and diced

1 whole lemon, cut into $1/4$-inch chunks

8 cloves garlic, peeled

4 large artichokes, prepared as opposite

1 cup olives

1 small bunch fresh thyme

$1^1/2$ cups water

1 teaspoon salt

1 teaspoon freshly ground black pepper

Pecan and maple glazed yams

New Zealand yams (originally from Peru—along with almost 3,000 types of potato!) have finally made it to London, where they're called chioca. They've become a firm favorite on the menu at The Providores when they're in season.

Serves 4

1 lb yams

3 tablespoons olive oil

salt and freshly ground black pepper

$^1/_2$ scant cup maple syrup

$1^1/_4$ cups pecan halves, lightly toasted

Preheat oven to 400°F. Line a roasting dish with baking paper. Cut yams lengthwise and toss with olive oil and some salt and pepper. Roast until almost cooked, 25 to 30 minutes. Add maple syrup and pecans to yams, mix them together, and return to the oven. Roast until yams begin to lightly caramelize. Gently toss again and serve straight from the oven.

Pumpkin, pine nut, and sage purée

This dish is excellent with white meat, especially grilled veal cutlets.

$1^1/_4$ lb peeled and seeded pumpkin, cut into
   $^3/_4$-inch cubes

3 tablespoons olive oil

1 clove garlic, peeled and quartered

$^1/_3$ cup boiling water

$^2/_3$ cup pine nuts, lightly toasted

8 sage leaves

3 tablespoons butter

salt and freshly ground black pepper

Preheat oven to 400°F. Toss pumpkin with oil and garlic and place in a nonstick or parchment paper–lined roasting dish. Pour over boiling water and roast 40 minutes, until tender. Transfer pumpkin and juices into a food processor with remaining ingredients and purée. Adjust seasoning to taste and serve hot.

Heat oil in a deep, heavy saucepan and add onion, carrot, lemon, and garlic cloves. Turn heat to full and cook everything for 4 minutes, gently stirring to prevent burning. Add prepared artichokes and carefully stir to coat with oil. Add remaining ingredients, bring to the boil, then cover and turn to a rapid simmer. Cooking times will depend on size of artichokes—those about 3 inches across will take 20 minutes to cook. They're done when you can just push a sharp knife through the base. Let cool and serve on a bed of salad greens with the braising vegetables inside the "choke."

How to prepare artichokes

Fill a large bowl with cold water and add juice of 2 lemons; this will prevent chokes discoloring. Hold your artichoke hoizontally and firmly by its stem on a cutting board and use a large, sharp, serrated knife to cut top $^2/_3$ off. This is the peaked end of the artichoke. Using a smaller sharp knife, trim thick outside leaves off and cut or snap the stem off at the base. Using a teaspoon, scoop out the hairy choke and discard it; this can be a little hard at first. Put artichokes in water until you're ready to use.

Oven-braised red onions, garlic, and rosemary

This dish is simple and versatile. It can be eaten as a warm starter on grilled crusty bread with a creamy goat cheese or served alongside roast meat or grilled fish. Onion rings cooked the same way are delicious served cold, tossed through a salad.

Serves 6

6 medium red onions

12 cloves garlic, unpeeled

2 tablespoons fresh rosemary leaves

$1/2$ cup balsamic *or* red wine vinegar

1 cup extra virgin olive oil

1 teaspoon salt

1 teaspoon freshly ground black pepper

Preheat oven to 400°F. Cut onions into quarters through the root, then peel off skin. Place in a ceramic roasting dish with all remaining ingredients and mix well. Cover tightly with a lid or foil and roast 1 hour, then remove foil and roast another 10 minutes. You can eat the onions straight away or let them cool in their juices. They keep, covered, in the fridge for 5 days.

Caramelized red onion tart tatin

This makes an unusual carbohydrate component for a meal—so you can skip the potatoes next time you're getting the Sunday roast ready. It's equally delicious served simply with a salad in summer or with some soft goat cheese crumbled on top once you remove it from the oven. I've found the best pan to make this in is a 12-inch non-stick ovenproof pan. Although it's also lovely made as individual tarts in small blini pans—you'll need to make four of those.

Serves 4 as a side dish

$1/4$ cup ($1/2$ stick) butter

4 medium red onions, peeled and cut into $1/2$-inch slices

1 tablespoon fresh thyme leaves

2 teaspoons sugar

1 puff pastry sheet, thawed

Preheat oven to 400°F. Grease the bottom of an ovenproof pan with the butter and lay the onion slices in it. Place over a moderate heat and fry until onions are colored, then gently turn over, scatter with the thyme and sugar, and cook again until onions are colored and softening.

Meanwhile, shape pastry in a circle (or a shape to match your pan) about 13 inches round and about $1/4$ inch thick. Once onions are done, lay pastry on top, tucking sides in. Bake until pastry is puffed and golden, about 15 to 20 minutes. Remove from oven and gently shake the pan, then invert it onto a plate and tip it out.

Eggplants stuffed with cracked wheat, tahini, and dill

The mixture used here as a stuffing is also good on its own or served with grilled meat or fish. I'm well aware that kirmizi biber and nigella seeds can be difficult to obtain, but don't fear—this will still taste great using the suggested alternatives.

Serves 4 as a main course

2 large eggplants

1 medium red onion, diced

3 tablespoons olive oil

$^1/_2$ teaspoon cumin seeds

$^1/_2$ teaspoon nigella seeds *or* black mustard seeds

$^1/_4$ teaspoon ground cinnamon

1 to 2 teaspoons kirmizi biber *or* chile flakes

1 cup cracked wheat

1$^1/_4$ cups boiling water

2 tablespoons pomegranate molasses *or* tamarind paste *or* balsamic vinegar

2 tablespoons tahini paste

1 large handful chopped dill

salt to taste

Preheat oven to 350°F. Split eggplants lengthwise (keep stalks on) and scoop out flesh to leave a $^1/_4$-inch-thick skin. Finely chop the flesh. Sauté onion in oil until golden, then add spices and cook until aromatic. Add cracked wheat and cook over a moderate heat for half a minute to coat it with the spices, then add eggplant and cook another minute. Add enough boiling water to just cover and mix well. Cook over a moderate heat until water is absorbed. Add more water and continue until wheat is just cooked, stirring frequently. Remove from heat and add pomegranate molasses, tahini, dill, and salt.

Lay eggplants in an oiled ovenproof dish, just large enough to hold them, and spoon filling into their cavities. Pour $^1/_2$ cup of hot water into dish, cover tightly with foil, and bake 25 minutes. Serve with a crisp green salad.

Eggplant, cabbage, lentils, and polenta with cheddar crumble

This can be made in one large dish or individual dishes if you prefer. Use the recipe as a guide and add whatever other yummy things you want—smoked bacon, blue cheese, sundried tomatoes—to the cabbage mixture. You can also replace the cheddar with parmesan or goat cheese.

Serves 6

olive oil for basting

1 large eggplant, cut into 1/4-inch slices

1/2 small cabbage (I prefer savoy), shredded

1 teaspoon dried oregano

1 cup water

salt and freshly ground black pepper

2 1/4 cups cooked lentils *or* canned lentils

3 1/3 cups vegetable stock *or* water

1 clove garlic, peeled and crushed

1 teaspoon salt

1 1/3 cups instant polenta

3 1/2 oz (about 1 cup) cheddar, grated

1/3 lb (about 4 to 5 slices) stale bread (I used 1-day-old focaccia)

Preheat oven to 400°F. Generously oil (or butter) an 8 x 8-inch lasagne dish. Lightly brush eggplant slices on both sides with a little oil and fry over a high heat until golden and just cooked. Put to one side.

Place cabbage, oregano, water, and a little salt and pepper in a deep saucepan and boil 2 minutes. Add lentils (and any other tasty extras you like), mix well, and remove from heat.

Bring vegetable stock and garlic to the boil in a saucepan, add 1 teaspoon of salt, then whisk in polenta and cook, stirring, over a low simmer for 1 minute.

Using a wet spoon, spread polenta over base and sides of the oiled dish. Add drained cabbage mixture and sprinkle with 4 tablespoons of cheddar. Lay eggplant on top.

Place bread in a food processor and grind to coarse crumbs. Add remaining cheese and process for a few seconds more. Sprinkle on top of eggplant, drizzle with a little more oil, and bake until golden, about 20 minutes. Serve piping hot.

Eggplants—to salt or not to salt?

Many people waste a lot of time salting eggplants before cooking them. Only in exceptional cases is it now necessary. Most commercially grown eggplants have no bitterness in them; it has been bred out of them. If you are growing eggplants in your own garden, next time you cook them, try one without salting—you may not need it. If you come across the small Thai eggplants, either the round white or green ones, you can usually remove their bitterness by cutting them into quarters, then soaking them in cold water for a few hours. Eggplants are such unusual vegetables anyway that sometimes the hint of bitterness, not quite expressed, adds to their charm.

Spicy eggplant with lemon roasted olives

Serve this with crisp, toasted pita bread and hummus for a superb starter. Eggplant also teams well with roasted red meat, and the olives are good in a mixed salad.

Serves 6 as a starter

1 cup large green olives, pit in

1 lemon, halved and finely sliced

2 cloves garlic, peeled and roughly chopped

2 teaspoons fennel seeds

$^1/_2$ cup olive oil

2 cups hot water

2 large eggplants, cut in $^1/_2$-inch discs

1 teaspoon ground cumin seeds

1 teaspoon ground fennel seeds

1 teaspoon ground cilantro seeds

$^1/_4$ teaspoon paprika

1 teaspoon salt

2 teaspoons brown sugar

Preheat oven to 400°F. Put olives, lemon, garlic, fennel seeds, and half the oil into a roasting dish just large enough to hold them and add the hot water. Roast 35 minutes until olive skins are beginning to shrivel and most of the water has evaporated. Stir every 10 minutes during this stage.

Meanwhile, brush remaining oil onto both sides of eggplants and lay the slices in a baking tray. Mix seeds, paprika, salt, and sugar together and sprinkle over the slices. Cook for 20 minutes, then test. They are cooked when a knife goes through easily. Let cool a little before removing from tray. To serve, simply place a few pieces of eggplant on a plate and scatter some olives on top. You can also sprinkle on generous amounts of chopped, fresh parsley, cilantro, and mint to give it a fresh taste.

Bacon-wrapped asparagus with radishes and butter

Delicious and simple. This dish started out as something quite different from this recipe, but when I teamed the radish and butter with the asparagus and bacon, I just had to write it down.

Serves 4

12 large asparagus spears

12 strips smoked bacon

12 radishes, washed

$^1/_4$ cup ($^1/_2$ stick) unsalted butter

coarse sea salt

Snap asparagus to remove woody stems or peel them. Lay a bacon strip on a cutting board and place an asparagus spear on top. Roll up tightly, then do the same to remainder. Place on barbecue in a moderately hot place, or in a hot skillet pan, and turn over once bacon is cooked on one side, being careful not to let it catch fire as the fat drips onto the coals. Serve on a plate with radishes, a blob of butter, and some salt.

Green banana and eggplant curry

Based on a Keralan vegetable curry, this dish is rich, light, and dense in flavor all at the same time. Kerela is a Southern Indian state, surrounded by waterways and palm trees, with the highest literacy rate in India. Its cuisine is the inspiration behind one of my favorite books, The God of Small Things *by Arundhati Roy. Curry leaves are pointed oval in shape and can be found at Indian markets and some Asian groceries. Green bananas, just like plantains, should only ever be eaten cooked—they can be used as the carbohydrate component of the meal, much like potatoes, but obviously with exotic over-tones. Cooked green bananas have a delectable texture similar to that of kumara.*

Serves 4

2 tablespoons peanut oil

2 teaspoons mustard seeds

1 teaspoon cilantro seeds

1 teaspoon cumin seeds

4 cardamom pods, lightly crushed

3 tablespoons shredded coconut

2 cloves garlic, peeled and crushed

1 teaspoon chile flakes *or* paprika

1 teaspoon salt

2 to 3 large green bananas *or* plantains, peeled and sliced into $1/2$-inch pieces

2 medium eggplants, cut into $3/4$-inch cubes

30 fresh curry leaves

1 scant cup vegetable stock

2 teaspoons tamarind paste

$1/2$ scant cup cream

3 tablespoons natural yogurt

juice of 1 lime *or* $1/2$ lemon

$1/4$ cup flaked almonds, lightly toasted

$1/4$ cup green onions, finely sliced

Heat oil in a deep saucepan, add seeds and cardamom, and fry over a moderate heat until aromatic. Add coconut, garlic, chile, and salt and gently fry until coconut is golden. Add bananas and fry 20 seconds, then add eggplants and curry leaves and fry another 20 seconds, stirring well. Add stock and tamarind paste and bring to a boil. Cover and simmer until bananas are just cooked, about 15 minutes. If the curry dries out, add some boiling water. Stir in cream and yogurt and bring to a simmer, then mix in lime juice and check seasoning.

Serve on basmati rice, cooked with a little lemon zest. Sprinkle curry with almonds and green onions.

Green banana and eggplant curry

Parsnip coconut curry

This is great eaten either as part of a vegetarian meal or with a simple roast meat or fish. The tomato paste adds color and a slight tang, but if you can find sundried tomato purée, then use that instead. You can also successfully replace some of the parsnips with carrots, rutabaga, or celeriac.

Serves 4

3 tablespoons peanut oil

2 cloves garlic, peeled and finely chopped

1 thumb fresh ginger, peeled and finely grated

2 red chiles, seeded and finely sliced

1 lemon grass stem, finely sliced

2 kaffir lime leaves, finely shredded

1 large onion, peeled and diced

$^1/_3$ cup tomato paste

1 (13.5-oz) can unsweetened coconut milk

2 lb parsnips, peeled and cut into $^3/_4$-inch cubes

1 small bunch cilantro, stems intact, washed well

3 tablespoons soy sauce

salt to taste

3 tablespoons lime juice

Heat oil in a deep saucepan, add next six ingredients, and fry until beginning to caramelize. Add tomato paste and fry, stirring well, for another 30 seconds. Next add coconut milk and parsnips, adding water to cover them, and bring to the boil.

Remove and reserve leaves from cilantro, then chop stems as finely as you can and add to curry. Turn curry to a simmer, cover the pot, and cook until parsnips are done. Mix in the soy, adding extra salt to taste, then remove from the heat. Just before serving, stir in cilantro leaves and lime juice.

Sesame and ginger broccoli

I like to serve this with roast chicken or grilled fish in summer or with roast pork in winter. Making it in a wok with a lid makes it easier, but a good frying pan works just as well. I have used a mixture of white and black sesame seeds for extra color and flavor.

Serves 4 as a side dish

> **1 tablespoon peanut oil**
>
> **2 medium heads broccoli, cut into individual florets**
>
> **1 thumb fresh ginger, peeled and finely chopped or grated**
>
> **3 teaspoons toasted sesame seeds**
>
> **3 tablespoons water**
>
> **1 teaspoon soy sauce**
>
> **1 teaspoon Thai fish sauce**
>
> **1 teaspoon sesame oil**

Heat a wok over a high heat and add oil. When it's smoking, quickly add broccoli and toss well with a pair of tongs. Cook until broccoli begins to color. Add ginger and sesame seeds and continue to cook 20 seconds, then add water, sauces, and sesame oil. Cover wok and cook on high heat for 1 minute only. Eat straight away, or let cool and have as a salad at room temperature.

Oven-dried tomatoes

This is a good way of using up surplus tomatoes when the thought of another roast tomato or fresh tomato salad is too much to bear. You can dry them and, when cooled, keep them in olive oil in the fridge for four to five days. They won't dry out totally but will be firm and slightly chewy. They are good eaten with cold meats, cut up into salads, tossed with pasta, or used to spice up a burger.

> **4 large ripe tomatoes**
>
> **salt and freshly ground black pepper**
>
> **superfine sugar (if tomatoes aren't very ripe)**

Preheat oven to 300°F. Place a cake rack on a baking tray and heat in oven for a few minutes. Cut the top and bottom off tomatoes, then slice them into 1/4-inch-thick slices with a sharp knife.

Lay them on heated rack, sprinkle with good salt (Maldon is my favorite) and cracked pepper. If tomatoes aren't too ripe, sprinkle with a little superfine sugar, too.

Place in middle of the oven and leave for 1 hour, then check. They should have firmed up, at which point you can turn them over and leave for another hour before removing from the oven. If they start to brown, turn heat down a little.

Cornish-style roasted turnips

Back in 1995 Michael and I, along with a "diverse" group of people, headed to Cornwall to celebrate Christmas. It was kind of odd, because on the south coast where we were staying it was balmy, whereas on the west coast it was snowing. We came across a field of turnips that had literally been frozen out of the ground, squeezed up and out by the frozen dirt. We picked so many and then had to come up with things to do with them—this was the best and easiest option, and it went with our roast duck superbly. Turnips have a delicate, peppery flavor. Rutabagas, to which they are sometimes likened, are a hybrid between a turnip and a cabbage—I bet you didn't know that! You can roast an assortment of root vegetables in the following way. Use "hard" herbs such as rosemary, sage, oregano, or thyme.

Serves 4

1¹/₄ **lb medium turnips**

2 **medium red onions**

¹/₄ **cup mixed fresh herbs**

¹/₄ **cup extra virgin olive oil**

7 **tablespoons butter**

salt and freshly ground black pepper

³/₄ **cup boiling water (from the kettle)**

Preheat oven to 400°F. Scrub turnips and cut into chunks. Peel and quarter red onions. Mix everything except the water together and place in a roasting dish just large enough to hold it all. Add water, then cover with a lid or foil and roast 1 hour. Remove lid, give vegetables a good mix, and continue roasting until they begin to caramelize.

Creamy mustard potato gratin

Potatoes are the world's best comfort food. With the addition of cream and mustard they will lift the humble sausage or lamb-chop dinner to another level.

Serves 6

2¹/₂ lb potatoes

7 tablespoons butter (reserve 1 tablespoon)

2 large onions, finely sliced

1 tablespoon chopped fresh rosemary *or* sage

2 teaspoons salt

freshly ground black pepper

2 to 3 large tablespoons hot English *or* Dijon mustard

2 cups cream

Preheat oven to 350°F. Peel or scub potatoes and slice ¹/₂ inch thick. Put in a deep saucepan and cover with cold salted water. Barely bring to a boil and drain.

Meanwhile, heat butter up in a deep saucepan and add onions. Cook over a moderate heat until wilted but not colored. Add herbs, seasoning, and mustard and cook 1 minute. Add cream and bring to a boil.

Rub remaining butter over the base of a deep 12-inch-square oven dish. Put in half the potatoes, pour in half the onion mixture, add remaining potatoes, then remaining onions. Seal with foil. Bake 40 minutes. Remove foil and cook until golden and potatoes are tender, about 20 minutes. Eat hot or save for the next day, and it'll taste even better when reheated.

Creamy anchovy and potato gratin

This is a new take on an old Swedish recipe called Jansen's Temptation. It is delicious eaten straight from the oven or even cold the next day.

Serves 6 to 8

  3 lb baking potatoes, peeled or scrubbed
  1 cup (2 sticks) butter, at room temperature
  3^1/$_2$ oz (about ^{2}/$_3$ cup) parmesan, finely grated
  2 cups cream
  3^1/$_2$ oz (about 18 to 22) anchovies in oil, roughly
    chopped
  1 cup chopped parsley
  salt and freshly ground black pepper

Preheat oven to 350°F. Cut potatoes into ^{1}/$_2$-inch slices and place in a large saucepan. Cover with cold water, add a few teaspoons of salt, and bring to a boil, then cook 6 minutes. Drain in a colander—they should be about half cooked and not mushy.

  Grease a 3-quart baking dish with half the butter and sprinkle with half the parmesan. Bring cream and remaining butter to the boil in a pot. Add anchovies, parsley, and salt and pepper to taste. Place half the potato slices in the bottom of the baking dish and pour on half the cream mixture. Add remaining potatoes and pour the rest of the cream on top, then sprinkle with remaining cheese. Cover the dish with a lid or foil and bake 35 minutes. Remove lid and cook until potatoes are tender and the crust is golden, about 20 to 25 minutes.

Baby beets with sherry vinegar and pecan dressing

This is really good served with grilled beef fillet, alongside horseradish mash (just make your creamiest mashed potatoes and add horseradish), with a whole baked snapper, or with a straight-from-the-oven goat cheese quiche.

Serves 4 to 6

  12 baby beets, about the size of large walnuts
  ^{1}/$_4$ cup sherry vinegar
  1 teaspoon sea salt
  ^{1}/$_2$ cup extra virgin olive oil
  1 cup pecan nuts, toasted and roughly chopped

Preheat oven to 400°F. Wrap beets, two at a time, in foil and place in a roasting dish. Bake until tender, about 60 minutes. (Test by pushing a skewer through the foil.)

  Cool beets to a temperature you can handle. Put on some gloves (to prevent staining hands), remove foil, and peel with either your fingers or a small, sharp knife. Halve beets and pour vinegar over and add salt. Toss well and let cool completely.

  Just before serving, pour oil over beets, add nuts, and toss it all together.

Creamy cauliflower and leek purée

This purée is equally as good to serve with the Sunday roast as it is with grilled tuna or mackerel. You can add finely grated parmesan or cheddar to give it an extra zing.

Serves 6 as a side dish

> 1 medium-large cauliflower, green leaves removed,
>   broken into pieces
> 1 large leek, washed and finely sliced
> 1³/₄ cups milk
> 1³/₄ cups water
> 1 bay leaf
> 1 clove garlic, peeled (optional)
> ¹/₂ teaspoon freshly ground white pepper
> salt
> cheddar *or* parmesan to serve (optional)

Place cauliflower, leek, milk, water, bay leaf, garlic, and pepper in a large saucepan. Cover and bring to a rapid boil. Turn to a moderate boil and cook 15 minutes, then remove lid and continue to cook until there is only ¹/₄ inch liquid left in the pot (this may take up to 15 minutes). Remove bay leaf and purée vegetables. Add salt to taste and cheddar or parmesan if desired.

Christmas mince roast kumara

This is a delicious accompaniment for roast turkey, duck, goose, or pork. (Pictured on page 157 with Roast Pork Belly à la Anna Hansen.)

Serves 6

> 1¹/₃ to 1¹/₂ lb kumara *or* sweet potatoes, skins
>   scrubbed, chopped into large chunks
> 3 tablespoons olive oil
> salt and freshly ground black pepper
> 3 tablespoons water
> ¹/₃ cup fruit mince

Preheat oven to 350°F. Line a roasting dish with parchment paper, and add kumara, oil, salt, and pepper. Mix together and then pour on the water. Roast until kumara are almost cooked. Gently mix in fruit mince. Continue cooking for about 10 minutes more, until kumara are done; you should be able to insert a knife easily into them as you would a potato.

Cabbage roasted with butter and garlic

I love to serve this with roast pork belly or braised venison haunch. It will work just as well with olive oil in place of the butter, too. For the photo, I stumbled upon some baby savoy cabbages, which I thought looked great, so hunt them out if you can.

Serves 6

1 large, 2 medium, or 3 baby cabbages (allow about
   $^1/_3$ lb per person)

1 cup (2 sticks) butter *or* $^2/_3$ cup olive oil

6 cloves garlic, peeled and sliced

$^2/_3$ cup boiling water

1 to 2 teaspoons coarse sea salt

freshly ground black pepper

Preheat oven to 350°F. Remove outside leaves and any damaged or dirty leaves from the cabbage. Cut stalk off at base of cabbage, then either cut into 6 to 8 wedges (large cabbage) or into halves or quarters (smaller cabbages). Heat a sauté pan and add butter and garlic. Cook over a moderate heat until garlic has turned golden.

   Add cabbage, cut sides down, and cook over a moderate heat 4 to 5 minutes until golden. Turn the cabbage wedges onto their other cut sides and cook for a minute longer, then add water and scatter salt on. Either place a lid on the pan or cover with foil and roast 4 minutes for the small cabbages or up to 13 minutes for the larger wedges. Remove from oven, grind on some fresh pepper, and serve piping hot.

rice, pasta, and noodles

Rice, pasta, and noodle dishes seem to appeal to almost everyone. I'm sure it's mostly to do with the comfort factor of the dishes. By cooking with rice, pasta, and noodles it becomes possible to spread a strong flavor base over a comforting medium. Pesto tossed through a cold salad is fine, but mixed through pasta or hot, diced potatoes it becomes flavorsome and enticing. Likewise, take away the rice or noodles from a nasi goreng or pad thai, and you're left with some strong flavors but no body. Those with a wheat intolerance, don't despair—in most recipes pasta can be replaced by Chinese rice noodles or spelt or buckwheat noodles.

Truffled leek risotto with seared scallops

There are some who say that a proper risotto shouldn't have parmesan added when it's served with fish. I disagree, as the parmesan adds a richness that complements many fish, but especially scallops, and it gives an "edge" to the rice, almost in the same way that lemon zest does, but in a more subtle way. However, you might want to serve it in a separate dish and let your guests decide.

Serves 8 as a starter

8 large or 24 to 32 small scallops, cleaned

2 tablespoons olive oil

salt and freshly ground black pepper

2 lemon grass stems *or* 1 teaspoon finely grated lemon zest

6 cups (1^1/$_2$ quarts) simmering vegetable stock

1 medium leek *or* white onion

^{1}/$_2$ scant cup extra virgin olive oil

2 teaspoons mixed fresh herbs (thyme, oregano, rosemary), chopped

1 lb risotto rice

2 teaspoons sea salt

^{2}/$_3$ cup finely grated parmesan

2 tablespoons truffle-infused oil

3 to 4 green onions, rinsed and finely sliced

2 limes for garnish

Brush scallops with oil and season with a little salt and pepper. Set aside at room temperature while preparing risotto.

Meanwhile, cut ^{3}/$_4$ inch from the base of the lemon grass, remove the outer 2 layers of stem, add both to the stock, and then finely slice the lower 2^1/$_2$–3 inches until it becomes too woody, placing any remaining bits in the stock. The more lemon grass in the stock, the more flavor. Finely slice and wash leek.

Heat oil in a large saucepan and sauté leeks and lemon grass over medium heat until very slightly golden. Add herbs and cook 1 minute. Add rice and salt and cook another minute, stirring well. Pour on half the simmering stock, stir well, then bring to a simmer and stir from time to time. Once the stock has been absorbed, add another ladle full, stir well, and let simmer until it needs more broth. Continue simmering, stirring, and adding broth as it is absorbed for about 20 minutes. Taste to check for doneness—it shouldn't be soft, but it mustn't be hard. If it is, add some more stock and continue to cook.

When rice is nearly ready, heat a heavy or nonstick frying pan to smoking point. Add scallops and cook no more than 60 seconds on each side (small ones will need only 20 to 30 seconds). Scallops are best served no more than medium rare as they can become quite rubbery if overcooked. Keep warm on a covered plate.

Just before serving, stir parmesan, truffle oil, and green onions into the risotto. Check seasoning, spoon onto plates, and place scallops on top. Garnish with lime wedges.

Leek and asparagus risotto

A risotto is actually quite simple to make. All it requires are good stock, quality rice (arborio, carnaroli, or vialone nano), genuine parmesan cheese, and about 25 minutes of your time. The asparagus in this recipe can be replaced with most other vegetables. The thing to aim for is a slightly al dente but creamy rice at the end of its cooking.

Serves 4 as a main course

5 to 6 cups (1¼ to 1½ quarts) simmering vegetable stock (simmer asparagus trimmings, garlic skins, carrots, herbs, and bay leaves in half water and half dry white wine for 25 minutes, then strain broth)

1 cup (2 sticks) unsalted butter

1 leek, washed and finely sliced

2 cloves garlic, peeled and finely sliced

1 onion, peeled and finely sliced

½ teaspoon fennel seeds

2 cups risotto rice

1 teaspoon salt

1 teaspoon freshly ground black pepper

1 bay leaf

2 teaspoons fresh thyme leaves

1 lb fresh asparagus, trimmed, ends used previously in stock and the rest sliced

1 cup parmesan cheese, grated, plus some extra for garnish

1½ tablespoons lemon juice

It is important that the stock is simmering at all times, so keep it on the stove close to the risotto pot. Heat a heavy saucepan and add three-quarters of the butter, the leek, garlic, onion, and fennel seeds. Stir gently and sauté until the onion is beginning to turn golden. Add rice, turn heat up to almost full, and fry for 1 minute, stirring well. Add salt, pepper, and herbs and stir well, then ladle on enough hot stock to cover rice by ½ inch (it will bubble furiously at first). Turn heat to low, stirring again. Once stock has been absorbed, add another ladle, stir for a minute, and leave again for stock to be absorbed. Keep cooking this way until the rice has cooked a total of 10 minutes.

Now add the sliced asparagus, another ladle of stock, stir well, and wait until stock is absorbed again. By now the risotto will almost be done. If you want it al dente it will probably be ready; if you want it cooked more and of a more liquid consistency, then add more stock, stir well, and continue cooking. Stir in the parmesan, remaining butter, and lemon juice and check seasoning. Eat piping hot with a little extra parmesan grated on top.

Gnocchi with tomato, olives, and garlic confit

Gnocchi are little dumplings made from potato, a little flour, and sometimes eggs. They are a great thing to have at hand as they take no time to cook (much like pasta), and they are filling when served with even a simple tomato and basil sauce. They always seem to sit next to the pasta in the Italian food aisle of the refrigerated section in the deli.

Serves 4 as a small main course

> 12 cloves garlic, peeled
>
> $3/4$ cup extra virgin olive oil
>
> 1 (28-oz) can chopped tomatoes
>
> 4 small bay leaves
>
> 1 large handful best-quality olives
>
> $1^3/4$ lb gnocchi
>
> 5 oz (about 1 cup) mozzarella, cut into chunks
>
> 1 handful chopped parsley

First make garlic confit, which can be done up to 10 days in advance. Place garlic in a small, heavy saucepan and cover with oil (add extra oil if necessary). Place over a very low heat and cook 1 hour or until soft and golden. (Too hot and the garlic will burn.) Let cool in the oil, then store (still in the oil) in the fridge, until ready to use.

Pour $1/3$ cup of the garlic oil into a wide, high-sided frying pan and bring to a high heat. Carefully pour in tomatoes (it will splatter a bit) and stir over a high heat for 1 minute. Add bay leaves, olives, and confit garlic (use the remaining garlic oil in other dishes). Continue cooking until sauce has thickened to the point where a spoon moved through it leaves a trail for a few seconds.

Meanwhile, cook gnocchi in boiling salted water to packet instructions.

Stir gnocchi, mozzarella, and parsley into sauce and serve.

Fish dumplings with vermicelli spikes and oregano and anchovy sauce

These are best served as a starter as the flavors are quite bold. Cod, hapuku, and snapper are suitable for the dumplings.

Serves 4 as a starter

Oregano and anchovy sauce

2 tablespoons fresh oregano

1 tablespoon fresh parsley

6 to 8 anchovies in oil, roughly chopped

1 teaspoon small capers in vinegar *or* salt, drained or rinsed

1 cup olive oil

juice of 1 lemon

1 lb fish fillet, skin and bones removed

2 cloves garlic, peeled and crushed

1 egg white

2 teaspoons fresh oregano

$1/2$ teaspoon lemon zest

salt and freshly ground black pepper

$1^2/_3$ oz vermicelli, crushed by hand to make $^3/_4$–$1^1/_4$-inch lengths

oil for cooking

To make the sauce, place oregano and parsley in a bowl with anchovies and capers. Stir in olive oil and lemon juice. Set aside at room temperature to develop flavors.

Place fish, garlic, egg white, oregano, and lemon zest in a food processor and pulse to a fine paste. Season to taste. Refrigerate for half an hour.

Divide mixture into 12 balls and roll in vermicelli to coat. Using your hands, squeeze noodles into fish to make them stick. Heat oil in a small frying pan. Add half the fish balls, cook until golden, flip over and cook for a further minute or so, then remove from oil with a slotted spoon and drain on absorbent paper. Cook remainder the same way.

To serve, spoon some sauce on a plate and place two or three fish balls on top.

Lemon, pine nut, raisin, and spinach pasta

This makes for a great luncheon or brunch dish, rich yet light at the same time, with a zing of lemon to counteract the sweetness of the raisins. Penne, linguine, or fusilli would all work equally as well in this dish.

Serves 4

2/3 lb dried pasta

1/4 cup extra virgin olive oil

2 medium red onions, peeled and sliced 1/8 inch thick

3/4 cup pine nuts

1/2 cup raisins

2 lemons

1/4 cup (1/2 stick) unsalted butter, at room temperature

2 large handfuls baby spinach

1 teaspoon sea salt

grated parmesan (optional)

Cook pasta in plenty of salted water until al dente. Drain in a colander.

Meanwhile, heat a frying pan over medium-high heat, add oil and onions, and cook 1 minute until onions soften. Add pine nuts and continue to cook until they become golden, then add raisins and cook until they begin to swell and caramelize, stirring frequently.

Peel rind off one lemon with a potato peeler and finely julienne it, then juice both lemons. Add lemon juice and zest to onion mixture and cook over medium heat 3 to 4 minutes, stirring well. Add butter and mix in well.

Transfer cooked and drained pasta into a large bowl and mix in spinach and salt, then the "sauce." Spoon into four bowls and add freshly grated parmesan.

Cannelloni stuffed with mushrooms and pork

You can use premade cannelloni for this or just roll up sheets of lasagne, as I do. I also like to make this with ground duck or chicken.

Serves 4

2 large onions, peeled and diced

4 cloves garlic, peeled and chopped

1/3 cup (51/3 tablespoons) butter

2/3 lb ground pork

1 teaspoon *each* chopped rosemary, sage, and thyme

1/2 teaspoon freshly grated nutmeg *or* ground star anise

1/2 lb medium portabello mushrooms, thickly sliced

2 teaspoons miso paste *or* tomato paste

1 cup wine (red *or* white, but not too sweet)

6 to 12 sheets of lasagne *or* 8 to 12 cannelloni tubes

1 (14-oz) can chopped tomatoes

1 cup crème fraîche

1/2 cup cream

31/2 oz (about 2/3 cup) parmesan, freshly grated

Sauté onions and garlic in butter until soft. Add ground meat and herbs and cook for a few minutes, stirring to break up lumps. Add nutmeg, mushrooms, miso, and wine; stir well. Bring to a simmer, cover, and cook 40 minutes.

Remove lid and cook until most of the liquid has evaporated, about 12 to 15 minutes. Season to taste.

Meanwhile, boil pasta until al dente. Drain and run cold water over until cool.

Turn oven to 350°F. Lay a sheet of pasta on a cutting board (you may need to cut it in half) and spoon some mixture into the center. Roll lengthwise into a tube and place in a lightly oiled roasting dish, big enough to hold all tubes snugly in one layer.

Bring tomatoes, crème fraîche, and cream barely to the boil in a small pan. Pour over pasta and sprinkle with parmesan. Bake until bubbling and golden.

Fusilli with kumara, chile, minted peas, and parmesan

Here's a real fusion of Italy and New Zealand and a double-starch treat as well. Any short stubby pasta will work with this—penne, shell pasta, farfalle, and the like. Frozen peas are fine, but in summer there's no excuse for not using fresh garden peas.

Serves 4

about 1 lb kumara *or* sweet potatoes, scrubbed and peeled

2 cups fusilli, uncooked

1¹/₂ cups peas

1 to 2 red chiles, finely sliced

2 cloves garlic, peeled and finely sliced

¹/₃ cup extra virgin olive oil

1 large handful mint, shredded

2¹/₂ oz (¹/₂ cup) freshly grated parmesan

freshly ground black pepper

Cut kumara into ¹/₂-inch cubes and place in a deep saucepan. Cover with cold water, add some salt, and cook until almost tender, about 13 minutes. Meanwhile, bring a saucepan of salted water to a boil and cook pasta until al dente. Just before kumara is ready, add peas to the pan and continue to cook until they're done, about 4 mintues. Drain in a colander and transfer to a large bowl. Drain pasta and add to bowl.

Sauté chiles and garlic in oil in a small frying pan until colored. Remove from heat, stir in mint, then pour over pasta and gently toss. Serve dredged with parmesan and black pepper.

Orecchiette with spinach and salmon

I love orecchiette (which supposedly resemble little ears— but I've never seen anyone's ears like them!) served in a broth, tossed with wok-fried crispy duck and enoki mush- rooms, or cold in a chicken and fava bean salad. However, this dish is great for a spring or summer brunch. Large shell pasta (conchiglie) also works well.

Serves 4

- **2 teaspoons salt**
- **1 lb salmon fillet, skin and bones removed**
- **$1/2$ lb orecchiette**
- **2 tablespoons olive oil**
- **2 teaspoons sesame oil**
- **2 red onions, peeled and finely sliced**
- **1 to 2 red chiles, finely chopped**
- **$4^1/2$ cups (about $1/2$ lb) fresh baby spinach, washed**
- **1 lemon, juice and finely grated zest, separated**
- **1 teaspoon freshly ground black pepper**
- **2 green onions, finely sliced and washed**

Bring 4 quarts of water to a boil in a large saucepan, add 2 teaspoons salt, and turn to a simmer. Add salmon and poach 4 to 5 minutes until just cooked—it may be easier to cut the fillet into three pieces for this. Remove with a slotted spoon and set aside on a warm plate. Bring water back to the boil, add pasta, and cook until al dente.

Meanwhile, heat a large wok or frying pan and add oils, red onions, and chiles. Cook over a moderate heat until onions begin to caramelize. Add spinach, lemon zest, and pepper and cook until spinach wilts, then remove from heat.

Once pasta is ready, drain and add to wok with lemon juice; toss well. Check seasoning, then divide between four bowls. Break salmon into chunks, scatter over pasta, and sprinkle with green onions.

Pasta with broccoli, spicy sausage, parmesan, and fried sage

Any pasta works with this recipe, as do most greens. I used trompetti pasta and purple sprouting broccoli, but shredded chard or Swiss chard, regular broccoli, or bok choy would work just as well, although you may need to adjust the cooking time.

Serves 4

1 lb pasta

$^1/_3$ cup olive oil

2 red onions, peeled and sliced

3 cloves garlic, peeled and sliced

$^2/_3$ lb spicy sausages, sliced (try chorizo *or* a paprika bratwurst)

24 sage leaves

2 cups (about $^3/_4$ lb) broccoli, trimmed and cut into florets

1 teaspoon salt

$^3/_4$ cup boiling water

oil for frying

$2^1/_2$ oz parmesan, freshly grated (about $^1/_2$ cup)

Bring a large saucepan of salted water to a boil, add pasta, stir, then boil uncovered until almost cooked (for dried pasta this will be about 8 minutes). Drain.

Meanwhile, heat olive oil in a large pan and fry onions and garlic over a high heat until they begin to caramelize. Add sausage slices and half the sage leaves and gently stir until sausage is partly cooked. Add broccoli, salt, and boiling water, mix well, and put a lid on the pan. Cook on high heat for 1 minute, then add pasta, mix well, and continue to cook on high until pasta and broccoli are cooked al dente.

While this is all cooking, heat a little oil in a small frying pan and when hot (350°F) add remaining sage leaves (do this in batches to avoid overcrowding). Fry until crispy, then drain on paper towels.

To serve, spoon pasta into bowls, shave or grate parmesan over pasta, and sprinkle with some sage leaves.

Pasta with broccoli, spicy sausage, parmesan, and fried sage

Sautéed kidneys with leeks, gin, and cream on pasta

In my opinion, veal kidneys make a nicer meal than lamb kidneys, but they aren't so readily available. However, if you do have them, just cut the walnut-sized pieces off the main "lump" and use as lamb kidneys.

Serves 6 as a starter

> 15 lamb kidneys, peeled
> $^1/_3$ to $^1/_2$ lb pasta *or* gnocchi
> 1 tablespoon light oil
> $^1/_4$ cup ($^1/_2$ stick) butter
> 1 medium leek, washed and finely sliced
> $^3/_4$ cup cream
> 6 tablespoons gin
> salt and freshly ground black pepper

First clean the kidneys. Hold one between your fingers on a cutting board with the white gristle facing up. Using a sharp knife, cut down, avoiding gristle. This will give you two flattish kidney-shaped halves, one with gristle attached. Cut gristle out using the point of a sharp knife. Do the same for remainder, to give you 30 kidney halves.

Bring a large saucepan of salted water to the boil and cook pasta. Drain, toss with oil, and keep warm.

Heat a large frying pan and add half the butter. Cook until almost nut-brown, then add kidneys, cut side down, and fry 30 seconds. Turn over, fry another 20 seconds, then transfer to a bowl with their juices. Keep the pan hot and add remaining butter and when it's melted add the leek and cook until wilted and beginning to color. Add cream and gin and boil to reduce, adding kidneys once it begins to boil. Cook until kidneys are just losing their pinkness. Check seasoning and spoon over pasta while still hot.

Spicy chicken wonton soup with shiitake mushrooms

Wontons are to Chinese food what ravioli is to Italian cuisine. You should be able to buy wonton wrappers from any Asian market, but make sure you buy the correct ones, not spring roll wrappers—it has happened. If you have a Japanese market near you, you could use gyoza wrappers instead.

Serves 4

4 shallots, peeled and finely sliced

1 red chile, finely sliced

1 chicken drumstick

sesame oil for frying

2 kaffir lime leaves *or* 1 teaspoon grated lime zest

3^1/$_3$ cups chicken stock

^{1}/$_3$ to ^{1}/$_2$ lb raw skinless chicken breast, roughly chopped

4 green onions, finely sliced

^{1}/$_4$ teaspoon finely grated fresh ginger

about 4 teaspoons Thai fish sauce

20 wonton wrappers

1 egg, beaten

6 fresh shiitake mushrooms, sliced *or* use dried ones soaked in warm water for 15 minutes; add soaking liquid to broth

1 small handful cilantro leaves

Fry shallots, chile, and chicken drumstick in a wide saucepan in a little oil until just beginning to color and crisp. Add lime leaves and stock and bring to a boil. Simmer 15 minutes or until chicken is cooked. Remove chicken and cool.

Let the broth simmer while you make wontons. Place chicken breast meat, half the green onions, ginger, and 1 teaspoon Thai fish sauce into a food processor and pulse to a fine mince. Lay wonton wrappers on a cutting board, four at a time, and brush with beaten egg on two sides. Place a marble-sized ball of the chicken mince on each one (you'll need 20 balls) and pinch the sides of each wonton together. Press firmly, to expel any air, and seal.

Remove flesh from drumstick and divide between four warm bowls. Bring the broth back to a boil, add shiitake mushrooms and wontons, and simmer for 5 minutes, then place five wontons in each bowl. Scatter over green onions and cilantro, drizzle with chile oil, and serve piping hot.

Chile oil

1 large red chile (remove seeds and membranes if you want less heat)

^{1}/$_2$ teaspoon salt

2 tablespoons light olive oil

1 teaspoon toasted sesame oil

Grind together chile, salt, and oils with a mortar or in a small blender.

Ramen noodles with creamed sesame corn, crisp tofu, and toasted walnuts

This is a subtly flavored starter that I once served to some friends from Istanbul—it almost made them rethink their opinion on tofu. Almost! In summer, make the corn purée from fresh sweet corn. In winter, canned corn works well.

Serves 4 as a starter

1 lb tofu, cut into 1-inch cubes

1 cup corn kernels

1 cup cream

2 green onions, sliced

2 teaspoons sesame seeds, toasted

1/3 heaping cup flour

1 teaspoon salt

1/2 teaspoon paprika (preferably smoked)

3 tablespoons peanut oil

1/4 cup walnut pieces, roughly chopped

6 oz ramen noodles, boiled until cooked, then drained and tossed in a little peanut oil

12 chives, finely sliced

Place tofu on paper towels for 30 minutes to extract some of the water. Meanwhile, put corn, cream, green onions, and sesame seeds in a small saucepan; bring to a boil and simmer, uncovered, until cream has reduced by half. Purée in a blender or small food processor, check seasoning, and keep warm.

Combine flour, salt, and paprika and use this to coat the tofu. Heat half the oil in a frying pan and cook half the tofu until golden on all sides. Remove to a warm plate and cook remaining tofu. Add the remaining oil and gently fry walnuts until just golden.

To serve, place a quarter of the corn cream onto each plate, then place a pile of noodles on top and then some tofu. Scatter with walnuts and sprinkle with chives.

Tagliatelle tossed with smoked salmon and caviar

Serve this rich, decadent pasta dish for brunch or a substantial starter. It takes just minutes to make.

Serves 4

  ¹/2 scant cup vodka

  ¹/2 scant cup cream

  ³/4 cup crème fraîche

  ²/3 lb tagliatelle

  3 tablespoons butter

  7 oz smoked salmon slices, cut into ribbons

  3 tablespoons caviar (sturgeon if you're feeling posh
     or salmon *or* trout)

  1 tablespoon chopped chives

  salt and freshly ground black pepper

Place vodka, cream, and crème fraîche into a wide deepish saucepan and bring to a boil. Turn to a simmer and cook until reduced by one-third.

Meanwhile, bring a large saucepan of salted water to a boil and cook tagliatelle until al dente. Drain in a colander, then transfer to a bowl.

Add butter to the creams and turn up heat. Gently mix in the salmon, then take off the heat and add half the caviar. Check seasoning, then pour over pasta and gently toss together.

Serve topped with remaining caviar, chives, and some freshly ground pepper.

Fava bean, tomato, and mussel linguine

This is a lovely spring lunch dish—very simple and colorful.

Serves 4

> 3 tablespoons extra virgin olive oil
>
> 1 red onion, peeled and finely sliced into rings
>
> 4 cloves garlic, peeled and finely sliced
>
> 1/4 lb fava beans, shelled
>
> 20 green-shelled mussels *or* 40 black mussels, cooked and removed from shells
>
> 2 large ripe tomatoes, diced
>
> 1 small handful small mint leaves
>
> 1/2 lb linguine, cooked until al dente

Heat olive oil, red onion, and garlic together in a deep saucepan until garlic turns golden brown. Add the fava beans and cook, stirring, until at least a quarter of them begin to pop open.

Add mussels and tomatoes and stir well, then cover pan and cook on high heat for 1 minute. Toss in mint and linguine. Place lid back on and cook on high for a further 20 seconds. Spoon into bowls and serve piping hot.

Linguine with minted pistachio pesto

Any pasta will work, but the texture and shape of linguine give it a better pasta-to-pesto ratio.

Serves 6 as a starter

> 1/2 to 3/4 cup shelled, raw pistachios
>
> 1 large handful fresh mint leaves
>
> 1 large handful parsley leaves
>
> 2 cloves garlic, peeled
>
> 3/4 cup extra virgin olive oil
>
> 5 oz (about 1 cup) parmesan, finely grated
>
> salt and freshly ground black pepper
>
> 1 lb linguine

Preheat oven to 350°F. Lightly toast pistachios, then cool. Place all but 12 pistachios in a food processor with mint, parsley, and garlic. Process 5 seconds. Add half the oil and process another 5 seconds. Add about two-thirds of the parmesan and remaining oil. Process 5 seconds. Check seasoning and add salt and pepper if desired. The flavor will get diluted once you add the pasta, so make it quite strong. Transfer to a large bowl.

Bring a large saucepan of salted water to a boil and cook pasta until al dente (8 to 10 minutes). Scoop out 3 to 4 tablespoons of cooking water and mix into the pesto in the bowl. Transfer pasta into a colander to drain and then into the bowl and toss with the pesto. Serve in bowls with remaining parmesan and pistachios sprinkled on top.

Zucchini, oregano, and almond linguine

An incredibly simple starter, this really does rely on the best olive oil and crisp zucchinis.

Serves 4

2 large zucchinis (green *or* yellow)

3 tablespoons best-quality extra virgin olive oil

1 clove garlic, peeled and sliced

2 small teaspoons dried oregano

$^1/_2$ lb linguine

3 tablespoons sliced almonds, toasted

juice of 1 lemon

$2^1/_2$ oz ($^1/_2$ cup) freshly grated parmesan

Bring a large saucepan of lightly salted water to a boil. Meanwhile, trim zucchinis and cut into long julienne or peel with a potato peeler into thin strips. Heat a frying pan and add half the oil, the garlic, and oregano and cook over a medium heat until garlic barely colors. Add zucchini and gently cook, tossing until it wilts.

Add pasta to boiling water and cook until al dente. Drain in a colander, then place in a bowl. Add zucchini and everything else from the pan, the almonds, lemon juice, remaining oil, and parmesan. Mix well. Check seasoning and serve while hot.

seafood

If I was ever marooned on a desert island, I'd just have to hope that it was in clean, unpolluted waters and I had landed with a fishing rod. Somewhere like Pulau Perhentian Besar on Malaysia's northeast coast, where I spent four days camping back in 1986. Maybe some fresh limes or lemons would help too, but no need for a fire, as a good slab of sashimi would be a treat. I'd find it really hard to get through life without seafood of any kind—it's simple to prepare and cook, and the flavor of almost everything from our oceans is terrific. I also love it because it's one of the most pleasing ingredients to cook at home or in a restaurant, whether it be a spankingly fresh wild sea trout, a snapping langoustine, or a bowl full of baby squid. However, it's hard not to become increasingly worried about overfishing and sustainability. It's amazing to think that despite 70 percent of the Earth's surface being covered with water, there are increasing problems regarding continued availability. So shop wisely, buy only the freshest, and try to keep an eye on what is currently a viable resource.

Crayfish and snow pea salad with lime dressing

"Snow pea" is the term used in New Zealand and Australia for what the French call "mange-tout." I must admit I prefer the name "snow pea," although the French name, meaning "eat everything," makes a lot of sense. This is a lovely summer starter, and you can also serve smaller portions on crostini as a sort of canapé. You will need about two medium crayfish. To rare-cook the crayfish, add to a deep saucepan of boiling salted water and boil ten minutes, then remove from the pot and cool.

Serves 6

- 1 large thumb fresh ginger, finely julienned
- 2 teaspoons superfine sugar
- 1/4 teaspoon salt
- 2 tablespoons lime *or* lemon juice
- 1 1/4 lb rare-cooked crayfish tailmeat, out of the shell
- 18 snow peas, blanched and julienned
- 1/4 cup mint leaves, picked off stem
- 1/4 cup light olive oil

Mix ginger with sugar, salt, and lime or lemon juice and let pickle for 20 minutes. Cut crayfish tail into 1/4-inch-thick slices and if you have any leg meat, add that too. Mix ginger mixture, snow peas, and mint together, then carefully mix in crayfish and oil, gently mix, and divide between six plates. Serve lightly chilled.

Scallop sashimi with chile-cilantro dressing

Raw scallops may seem a bit too strange for some, but think of how good a raw oyster is and then try this—it won't taste as odd as you think. Try to find scallops with the red-orange coral attached.

Serves 4 as a starter

- 1/2 fresh mild red chile, finely sliced (remove seeds if you don't like the heat)
- 2 tablespoons lime juice *or* lemon juice
- 1 tablespoon sesame oil
- 2 tablespoons olive oil
- 1 tablespoon light soy sauce
- 8 large scallops (about 3/4 to 1 lb)
- 1 small handful cilantro leaves
- 1 teaspoon sesame seeds, toasted

Place chile, juice, oils, and soy sauce in a screw-top jar and shake well. Let stand for at least 20 minutes.

Clean scallops and remove coral if attached and set aside. Slice white meat into thin rounds, about 1/4 inch thick if possible. Lay slices, in one layer, on four plates. Chop coral into a fine mince and place in the center of the plates. Shake dressing again, then drizzle it over scallops. Scatter cilantro and sesame seeds on top and serve.

Seared tuna with sweet and sour onion relish

Tamarind is the seed pod from a beautiful tree in Southeast Asia and India. It has a sour, tongue-puckering taste and is extremely refreshing. You can find it in most Indian food shops. Make sure you choose line-caught tuna whenever possible. This also works really well made with mahi mahi or swordfish.

Serves 4

salt and freshly ground black pepper

4 (6-oz) pieces tuna loin, about 1 inch thick

1/3 cup olive oil

4 medium red onions, finely sliced

4 cloves garlic, peeled and finely sliced

4 limes, zest and juice

2 tablespoons palm sugar *or* superfine sugar

3 tablespoons tamarind paste

2 teaspoons Thai fish sauce

1/2 cup cilantro leaves

8 large basil leaves

Lightly season the fish and brush with a little oil. Let rest at room temperature while you make the relish. Heat the remaining oil in a deep frying pan and sauté the onions on a medium heat for 5 minutes, stirring occasionally. Once they begin to color, add garlic and turn heat up to high. Stir continuously for a minute, then add lime zest and juice, sugar, tamarind paste, and Thai fish sauce. Cook another minute, then stir in cilantro and basil leaves. Remove from heat.

Heat a griddle iron, skillet, or heavy frying pan until really hot and smoking. Place tuna on and cook for only 45 seconds each side. The fish will be rare and moist inside. Transfer to a plate and top with hot relish. Serve with crunchy steamed greens or a green salad.

Flounder and asparagus rolls in chile, lemon grass, and ginger broth

In theory this is similar to a Thai sour soup with poached fish. It's great served with a dish of rice or some cold noodles on the side as a light supper dish. You can make it in one large dish or individual dishes—I've opted for the latter.

Serves 4

2 medium flounder *or* sole, filleted but with skin on (keep bones for the stock but rinse them well)

4 cups cold water

1 small onion, peeled and sliced

2 lemon grass stems (chop off the bottom 3/4 inch and remove outer 2 to 3 layers and reserve trimmings for the broth)

16 medium asparagus (snap thick ends off)

1 teaspoon salt

4 kaffir lime leaves *or* the peel of 1 lime

1 large thumb fresh ginger, peeled and finely sliced

1 clove garlic, peeled and finely sliced

1 teaspoon sugar

2 green onions, finely sliced at an angle

1 handful cilantro leaves

1 red chile, finely sliced

2 juicy limes *or* lemons

Thai fish sauce to serve

Preheat oven to 350°F. Place fish bones in a large pot with water, onion, lemon grass trimmings, asparagus ends, and salt. Bring to the boil and simmer very gently with a lid on for 15 minutes. Strain through a fine sieve into a clean saucepan.

You will have four double fillets; cut each fillet in half lengthwise to give you eight single fillets. Break each asparagus stem in half. Lay fish fillets on a board, skin side down, and place two asparagus tips and two bottoms on each, then roll up. Start with the fat end and roll toward the tail. Secure tail end with a toothpick. If the skin is tough, cut a tiny hole with a sharp fine knife so you can get the toothpick in.

Place four wide ovenproof soup bowls on a tray in the oven. Finely slice lemon grass into rings until it begins to feel a little woody. Discard woody bits. Place fish stock back on the heat and add lemon grass, lime leaves, ginger, garlic, and sugar. Simmer 2 minutes.

Take bowls from the oven and divide soup and remaining aromatic ingredients between them, then sit two fish rolls in each. Bake around 5 minutes. The fish is cooked when it is opaque in the middle. Serve the Thai fish sauce separately and let your guests help themselves.

Baked fish and mussels with wine and potatoes

Cod, mahi mahi, large snapper fillets, or any meaty fish is suitable for this chunky stew. Clams or scallops (out of the shell) make a fine replacement for the mussels.

1³/₄ lb small potatoes, washed and cut into quarters or small wedges

1¹/₄ cups dry white wine

1 scant cup water

6 tomatoes, cut into wedges

2 cups fresh *or* frozen peas

¹/₂ cup extra virgin olive oil

1 cup basil leaves

6 (7-oz) fish fillets, bones removed, skin on

²/₃ lb mussels, washed and beards removed

salt and freshly ground black pepper

Preheat oven to 450°F. Place potatoes in a pot, add wine and water, cover, and bring to a boil. Cook 6 to 8 minutes until almost done. Add tomatoes and peas and gently stir, then take off the heat.

Drizzle oil into a roasting dish (I find a ceramic dish works best for this), sprinkle with basil leaves, then lay fish in, skin side up. Scatter mussels around the fish and spoon potato mixture over it all. Season with salt and pepper. Cover dish with a lid or foil and bake 10 minutes. Remove lid and continue to cook until fish is done and mussels are open—discard any that don't open. The fish is cooked when it is opaque in the center, although fish slightly undercooked is preferable to overcooked fish. Think sushi—raw fish is tasty! The easiest way to check the doneness of fish is simply to cut into the fattest part of the fillet and pull it back.

Serve hot from the oven in winter or at room temperature on a balmy day.

The simplest snapper sashimi

During a visit to filmmaker and vineyard-owner friend Michael Seresin in New Zealand's scenic Marlborough Sounds a few years back, I was fortunate to be given a freshly caught snapper. In the cupboard of the cabin where I was staying, I found some wasabi paste and soy sauce, and in the garden lemon trees were in fruit. The result: snapper sashimi.

Serves 4

1 small–medium snapper, about 1¹/₄ lb

1 teaspoon wasabi paste or powder

¹/₃ cup light soy sauce

juice of 1 lemon

All you do is fillet the fish, removing the skin, scales, and bones, and cut it against the grain into ¹/₄-inch-thick slices.

Mix the wasabi paste or powder into the soy sauce, then squeeze in the lemon juice. Dip the fish into this and enjoy.

Pan-fried salmon and chorizo with tomato and basil

Pan-fried salmon and chorizo with tomato and basil

Tomato and basil are a perfect pair, but I think salmon and spicy chorizo are also a great couple. To serve this as a main course (for two) rather than a starter (for four), you'd be best to make a salsa from the tomato and basil— just chop the tomatoes and tear the basil, then mix with the olive oil and lemon juice.

Serves 4 as a starter

> 3 tablespoons extra virgin olive oil
>
> 1/3 to 1/2 lb chorizo, cut into 8 slices
>
> 1 lb salmon fillet, bones removed, cut into
>   8 pieces, and lightly seasoned
>
> juice of 1 lemon
>
> 8 cherry tomatoes, halved
>
> 8 basil leaves

Heat 1 tablespoon of the olive oil in a frying pan over a moderate heat and sauté chorizo slices on both sides until colored. Remove to a warm plate.

Add another tablespoon of oil to the pan and add the salmon pieces, skin side down. Cook over a moderate-high heat for 1 minute, then turn and cook about 30 seconds—ideally the salmon should be quite rare. Take salmon out and take the pan off the heat, then add remaining olive oil and lemon juice and stir to loosen the crunchy bits.

To serve, divide salmon pieces between four plates, sit a chorizo slice on top of each piece, then place tomato halves and basil leaves on top. Drizzle with the pan juices.

Salmon baked with tomato, ginger, chile, and pineapple salsa

The oiliness of salmon takes well to this slightly fruity mixture. Serve this with something simple like boiled potatoes, rice, couscous, or just a green salad.

Serves 4

> 4 ripe tomatoes, cut into 1/2-inch cubes
>
> 1/2 thumb fresh ginger, peeled and finely julienned
>   or grated
>
> 1/2 red chile, finely julienned or chopped
>
> 1/3 to 1/2 lb fresh pineapple, skin removed,
>   finely diced
>
> 3 tablespoons olive oil
>
> 2 tablespoons soy sauce
>
> 4 (6-oz) pieces salmon fillet, skin and bones removed

Mix everything except salmon together in a bowl. Place salmon pieces in a ceramic roasting dish just large enough to hold them comfortably and pour salsa over and around them. Let marinate for 1 hour.

Preheat oven to 450°F. Place dish in top third of the oven and bake 15 minutes, then test to see if salmon is cooked. Ideally, it should be pink in the middle.

Serve salmon with salsa spooned around it.

Salmon, watercress, and wasabi guacamole burger

A burger doesn't have to have a ground beef rissolé in it—it needs a good bun, a great filling, and the possibility to dribble down your chin. Then you have a great burger!

Serves 2

1 (6$^1/_2$-oz) salmon fillet, skin and bones removed

salt and freshly ground black pepper

2 teaspoons sesame oil

1 ripe avocado

$^1/_2$ teaspoon wasabi paste or more to taste

2 teaspoons lemon juice

$^1/_2$ teaspoon salt

2 white sesame buns

1 handful watercress

1 small red onion, peeled and finely sliced into rings

Cut salmon into four pieces, lightly season, and brush with sesame oil. Halve avocado and scoop out flesh. Mash with wasabi, lemon juice, and $^1/_2$ teaspoon salt.

Heat a heavy or nonstick frying pan and cook salmon 40 seconds over a high heat, then turn and cook another 30 seconds. The salmon will be pink, almost raw inside. If you prefer it cooked more, turn heat to medium and cook up to 2 minutes on each side.

Split the buns and spread with avocado mash on both tops and bottoms. Place watercress on the bottoms, then two pieces of salmon, then finally the onion and replace the tops.

Salmon, watercress, and wasabi guacamole burger

Salmon and blue cod stew with aïoli

Blue cod is one of Australasia's loveliest fish; if you can't find it, use a good firm white fish. This can be made with any fish or shellfish, but cooking times may need to be adjusted accordingly. This is easy to make on top of the stove as it doesn't take too long to cook. It is delicious served cold in summer.

Serves 4

2 tablespoons extra virgin olive oil

2 medium red onions, peeled and cut into eighths

1 clove garlic, peeled and finely chopped

1 bay leaf

$1/4$ teaspoon saffron (optional)

$1/2$ lemon, juice and zest

$3/4$ cup canned peeled tomatoes *or* fresh tomatoes, chopped

1 cup white wine (a sauvignon blanc would be good)

2 teaspoons fresh thyme

salt and freshly ground black pepper

1 lb salmon fillet, cut into $3/4$-inch chunks

1 lb large blue cod fillet, cut into $3/4$-inch chunks

$1/4$ cup fresh oregano leaves

aïoli (recipe on page 43)

Heat a heavy, deep saucepan, then add olive oil and onions and sauté 5 minutes, stirring well, to color. Add garlic, bay leaf, saffron, and lemon and cook over moderate heat for 10 minutes, stirring to prevent it from sticking. Add tomatoes, wine, and thyme and bring to a boil, turn to a simmer, and cook with a lid on for 15 minutes. Check seasoning.

Add the fish pieces to the pan and mix in gently, then cook on a gentle simmer for 6 to 8 minutes until just done. Fish should still be a little undercooked. Remove fish from pan and place in a bowl. Add oregano to pan and bring to a boil again. Stir well and spoon over fish.

Serve with plain boiled or mashed potatoes and a separate bowl of aïoli on the side.

Steamed salmon with asparagus, ginger, and basil

Snapper, monkfish, or crayfish can be used in place of the salmon, and green beans can replace the asparagus. Serve with boiled new potatoes.

Serves 4

- 1 teaspoon finely chopped fresh ginger
- 1/2 teaspoon finely grated lemon zest
- 1 teaspoon roasted sesame oil
- 1/2 teaspoon salt
- 4 (6-oz) pieces salmon fillet (avoid tail end), skin and bones removed
- 1 lb asparagus spears
- 1 whole lemon, finely sliced
- 1 teaspoon salt
- 2 tablespoons extra virgin olive oil
- 1 small handful fresh basil, shredded
- juice of 1 lemon

Combine ginger, lemon zest, sesame oil, and 1/2 teaspoon salt and rub into salmon. Bring a saucepan of water to a hearty boil. Snap ends off the asparagus and add the ends to the pan along with lemon slices and 1 teaspoon salt. Sit a steamer on top and place a plate inside, large enough to hold the fish comfortably but with at least a 3/4-inch gap between the edge of the plate and the steamer. Cover and boil 2 minutes. Drizzle olive oil onto the plate, place the salmon on top, season with a little salt, and replace lid. Steam 2 minutes.

Scatter asparagus spears and basil over fish. Continue cooking for 2 minutes. To test if the fish is cooked, use a sharp knife to cut through the thickest piece—it should be barely translucent.

Remove plate from steamer, making sure not to spill the juices. Divide asparagus between four plates, place a piece of salmon on top, then spoon the juices from the plate and the lemon juice over the top.

Grilled swordfish on cucumber, peanut, and mint salad

Firm, meaty swordfish (or try hapuku, line-caught tuna, or mahi mahi) is perfect for grilling, so try this recipe on the barbecue in summer or at other times of the year use a heavy skillet or nonstick frying pan.

Serves 4

- 1/2 cup unsweetened coconut cream
- 1 handful cilantro leaves, shredded
- 1 teaspoon cumin seeds, lightly toasted
- 1/4 cup lime juice *or* lemon juice
- 1 teaspoon salt
- 4 (6-oz) thickish swordfish fillets (too thin and the dish will become dry)
- 1 large cucumber, julienned or coarsely grated
- 1 teaspoon superfine sugar
- peanut oil for cooking
- 1/4 cup mint leaves
- 1/4 cup roasted peanuts, crushed

Combine coconut cream, cilantro, cumin, lime juice, and salt. Add swordfish and mix. Place in a ceramic dish and refrigerate, covered, for 4 to 12 hours, turning occasionally. An hour before serving, combine the cucumber, sugar, and lime juice and set aside.

Five to 10 minutes before serving, drain fish from the marinade (discard the marinade) and pat dry, then brush with a little peanut oil on both sides. Either barbecue, grill, or fry fish until browned on one side, then turn over and cook until golden on the other side. It should take only a minute or two on each side, but this will depend on the thickness of the fish. Mix mint and peanuts into cucumber and divide it between four plates, then place fish on top.

Olive oil–poached cod with Mediterranean salad

Poaching fish in oil keeps it moist and juicy and preserves it for up to four days. Make this a few days ahead, but make the salad on the day. Tuna, hapuku, and snapper also work well. Use any leftover oil for tossing through pasta with fish or for grilling fish on the barbecue. Caperberries, sometimes called capernuts, are the pickled fruit from the caper bush. If they are unavailable, use green olives instead.

Serves 4

4 (5-oz) pieces cod, skin and bones removed

4 cups extra virgin olive oil

1 handful fresh basil leaves

Pat fish dry on paper towels. Place oil in a pan just large enough to hold the fish, but with enough room so that the pieces don't touch each other. Place on the stove and warm oil until tepid. Add basil leaves and try to make them settle on the bottom of the pan. Place fish on top and turn the heat up. You may need to add a little more oil so that it covers the fish. Bring to a very gentle simmer and cook until fish is barely done, about 8 to 12 minutes, depending on the thickness of the fish.

To test, carefully lift a piece out with a slotted spoon and pull back the flesh with a sharp knife—it should be translucent. You can serve it now or allow it to cool completely in the oil. Remove the fish with a slotted spoon, reserve the oil, and serve the fish with the salad.

If making this in advance, store the fish in the oil, covered tightly in the fridge. Bring back to room temperature before serving.

Mediterranean salad

1^1/$_2$ cups (about ^{1}/$_2$ lb) green beans, blanched and refreshed in cold water

1 large handful best-quality black *or* green olives

1 small handful flat-leaf parsley

2 tablespoons capers

2 tablespoons caperberries

2 limes and sea salt to serve

Toss beans, olives, parsley, capers, and caperberries with ^{1}/$_4$ cup of the poaching oil. Serve with a lime half and some sea salt.

Baked hoki steaks with tomatoes, pine nuts, and red onions

Saffron and tomato give fish dishes a real Mediterranean feel—the bouillabaisse factor. This is nothing like, and not as complicated as, bouillabaisse, but it would probably benefit from the addition of a few fresh shellfish: mussels, cockles, or New Zealand pipi. Serve it with lots of bread to mop up the sauce.

Serves 4

4 (7-oz) hoki *or* hake steaks, on the bone

$1/4$ cup extra virgin olive oil

2 medium-large red onions, peeled and finely sliced

$1/4$ cup pine nuts, lightly toasted

pinch saffron

4 large, ripe tomatoes, cut into small wedges

$1/4$ teaspoon ground allspice

1 handful fresh basil leaves

1 scant cup dry white wine

salt and freshly ground black pepper

Preheat oven to 400°F. Place a ceramic baking dish, just large enough to hold all the fish in one layer, in the oven. In a medium frying pan, heat half the oil and fry onions until they begin to caramelize. Add pine nuts, saffron, tomatoes, allspice, and basil and fry for 1 minute, then add wine and bring to a boil. Remove from heat and add salt to taste.

Brush fish with remaining oil and season with salt and pepper. Place fish in the hot baking dish and then pour onion mixture on top. Bake until fish is just cooked. It should take no more than 8 minutes.

Steamed fish and bacon wontons with sweet chile sauce

This is a take on a traditional Chinese dim sum, in which I've replaced air-dried pork with bacon. You can use any white fish as long as all bones and skin are removed—I used prawn meat. The mixture will keep in the fridge for two days.

Serves 5 as a starter

$2/3$ lb white fish, finely chopped

$1/4$ lb sliced smoked bacon, cooked until crisp, cooled, and finely chopped

$1/2$ teaspoon fresh ginger, finely grated, *or* candied ginger

3 to 4 smallish green onions, finely sliced; use all of the green

6 large mint leaves, finely shredded

1 teaspoon Thai fish sauce *or* $1/2$ teaspoon salt

10 (3 to 4 inches) square wonton wrappers

Combine fish, bacon, ginger, green onions, mint, and Thai fish sauce. Lay wonton wrappers on a work surface and divide mixture among the wrappers. Fold the corners into the center, pressing hard to make them stick to the mixture.

Lightly oil a plate, set it in a hot steamer, and place the steamer on a pot of boiling water. Place wontons on the plate, cover, and cook over a rapid boil 6 to 8 minutes. To test if they're cooked, insert a fine knife—it should come out clean. To serve, place wontons on a plate with a bowl of Simple Sweet Chile Sauce on the side.

Simple sweet chile sauce

$1/2$ cup demerara *or* raw sugar

3 tablespoons white vinegar

3 tablespoons soy sauce

2 red chiles, seeded and finely sliced

Bring all ingredients to a boil, then simmer for 2 minutes.

(Photograph of recipe on page 7.)

Italian sweet-pickled fish

I first made this classic Neapolitan dish back in 1989 at a restaurant I worked in called Friths in London's Soho, which chef Carla Tomasi owned. I tend to make this dish with whole anchovies or baby mackerel or sardines, but red mullet, gurnard, and snapper fillets work well too. Use either six fillets from three large fish, or twelve smaller fillets from six fish. Scale the fish but keep the skin on and remove the bones from the larger fish. I serve it as a starter, on toasted sourdough and undressed watercress with the pickling vegetables on top. It keeps in the fridge for a week and is actually better the day after it's made.

Serves 6 to 8 as a starter

1³/4 lb fish fillets (see above)

¹/3 cup flour

2 teaspoons salt

¹/2 teaspoon freshly ground black pepper

2 medium red onions, peeled and sliced into rings

¹/3 cup extra virgin olive oil

few sprigs of fresh thyme

1 bay leaf

2 heaped tablespoons dried currants

¹/3 cup demerara *or* raw sugar

1 scant cup cider *or* white wine vinegar

1¹/4 cups water

oil for deep frying

Pat fish dry with paper towels, then dust with flour mixed with 1 teaspoon salt and ¹/2 teaspoon pepper. Leave on a plate while you do the next step.

Fry onions in olive oil, stirring them occasionally, until they begin to caramelize. Add herbs and currants and fry 30 seconds. Add sugar, vinegar, and 1 teaspoon salt and boil 20 seconds. Add water, bring to a boil, then remove from heat.

Heat ³/4 inch oil in a saucepan to 350°F (a 12-inch-wide pan is ideal). Fry fish (in batches) for 90 seconds, or until golden brown. Drain on paper towels.

Spread half the onion mixture in the bottom of a nonreactive casserole dish and lay fish pieces on top, trying not to overlap them too much. Add remaining onions, then pour liquid on top. Ideally, the liquid will just about cover the fish. Let cool, then cover tightly in plastic wrap and refrigerate for at least 12 hours.

Mixed fish tartare with grilled bell pepper and zucchini julienne

This is a good way to use up bits and pieces of fish, as long as they're really fresh. It's delicious made with just one type of fish, although I used a mixture of snapper, cod, and wild sea trout.

Serves 4

1 lb (filleted and skinned) fish, bones removed, cut into 1/4-inch cubes

1 tablespoon baby or regular-sized capers, roughly chopped

1 tablespoon tapenade *or* olive paste

6 to 8 fresh mint leaves, shredded

6 large, fresh basil leaves, shredded

1 green onion, finely sliced

2 tablespoons lemon juice

1/4 teaspoon salt

1/2 teaspoon freshly ground black pepper

2 medium zucchinis

2 red bell peppers

2 tablespoons extra virgin olive oil

Mix fish with capers, tapenade, mint, basil, green onion, lemon juice, salt, and pepper. Cover and refrigerate 1 hour.

Trim both ends off zucchinis, then slice or peel off green skin lengthwise. Discard the white core. Lay skin on a cutting board and julienne it. Bring a deep saucepan of salted water to the boil and add zucchinis, count to 30, then drain into a colander. Refresh under cold water and drain again.

Roast and peel bell peppers (see page 15 for method), remove the stems, then cut into thin strips. Combine with zucchinis and mix. Remove fish mixture from the fridge 30 minutes before you want to serve it and mix; taste for seasoning.

To serve, mix fish one more time, then divide between four plates. Take a quarter of the salad mixture and twist it into a spiral. Place one spiral on top of each portion of fish and drizzle with olive oil.

Steamed scallops with buttered leeks, capers, and sherry vinegar

This recipe is fairly straightforward, and the simple flavors really shine through. It's important that the scallops are really fresh and not soaked in water—as these will just shrivel up and make the leeks very sloppy. Ask your fishmonger for unsoaked scallops, cleaned, and with the coral intact, if available.

Serves 2 as a starter

> 1 medium leek, sliced into 1/8-inch rings, rinsed well
> 3 tablespoons butter
> 2 tablespoons sherry vinegar *or* balsamic vinegar *or* lemon juice
> salt
> 4 to 6 scallops (depending on size)
> 1 tablespoon extra virgin olive oil
> 1 teaspoon capers, drained
> 1/4 teaspoon salt
> 1/4 teaspoon ground black pepper

Sauté leek in butter until soft and just beginning to color. Add vinegar and a little salt and cook over a high heat until vinegar has almost evaporated.

Bring a deep saucepan of water to a rapid boil, place a steamer on top with a plate inside, and cover. Mix scallops with oil, capers, and a little salt and pepper. Place leek mixture on plate in the steamer, then set scallops on top, placed apart to allow even cooking. Cover and cook until done. Small scallops will take up to 90 seconds, with ones the size of a walnut taking around 4 minutes. They are cooked when they're just opaque inside—any more and they can be too chewy. Remove plate and serve hot, straight away, with warm, buttered bread.

Scallop and fish pie with a potato crust

Most types of fish and shellfish will work well in this pie; just make sure there are no bones or shells. I like to make this using sweet potato mash instead of regular potatoes—see what you think.

Serves 4

> 1 2/3 lb potatoes, peeled and cut into 1 1/2-inch chunks
> 1/4 cup fresh tarragon leaves
> 1 teaspoon salt
> 1/4 cup extra virgin olive oil
> 1 teaspoon paprika
> 1 large leek, washed and finely sliced
> 3 tablespoons butter
> 1 large lemon, zest and juice
> 2 heaped tablespoons cornstarch mixed with 3 tablespoons cold water
> 1 1/2 tablespoons Thai fish sauce *or* 1 teaspoon salt
> 8 large scallops (cleaned, coral attached)
> 1 2/3 lb fish meat, skinned and boned, cut into 3/4-inch chunks
> 5 green onions, finely sliced

Preheat oven to 350°F. Boil potatoes with half the tarragon and salt until cooked. Drain into a colander, then put back in the pot with remaining tarragon and mash with olive oil and paprika.

Fry leek in butter until wilted, then add lemon zest and juice, cornstarch paste, and Thai fish sauce. Stir until thickened, then gently mix in scallops, fish, and green onions. Check seasoning, adding salt and pepper if needed. Place mixture in a lightly buttered 2-quart pie dish.

Roughly spread the mash on top of the fish; if you make it too smooth, it won't have that lovely rustic look that gives a crunchy texture. Bake until golden, around 30 minutes. Serve while still hot.

Grilled prawns with mango and fig salsa

While this salsa is terrific in the middle of summer, you may want to make it in winter when there are no fresh figs of any flavor. If so, use dried figs and add to the onion and citrus juice and let marinate for two hours. The prawns are best left to marinate overnight, so plan ahead to get this ready.

Serves 6

12 prawns, uncooked, in the shell

2 cloves garlic, peeled and crushed

1 thumb fresh ginger, finely chopped or grated

3 tablespoons sesame oil

1 red onion, peeled and finely diced

juice of 2 lemons *or* 3 limes

1 teaspoon finely grated lemon *or* lime zest

$^1/_2$ teaspoon salt

1 ripe mango, peeled and diced

3 ripe tomatoes, diced

$^1/_3$ to $^1/_2$ cup extra virgin olive oil

2 large fresh figs, stems removed and diced

Place prawns in a bowl with garlic, ginger, and sesame oil. Mix well and let marinate from 6 to 24 hours.

To make salsa, mix onion with citrus juice, zest, and salt and stand at least an hour, then mix in mango and tomatoes and stand another hour. Finally, mix in olive oil and figs.

Wipe excess marinade from prawns. Heat up the barbecue, grill, or heavy-bottomed frying pan and cook prawns 1 to 2 minutes each side depending on the size. (The shell acts as insulation at first, but once it heats up it becomes more like a kiln, and they cook very quickly.)

To serve, put a large platter of the prawns in the middle of the table, along with the salsa and finger bowls.

Yellow mussel, cockle, and potato curry

This is one of those dishes where I had no idea what was going to be produced as I began to cook it. It turned out to be delicious. The mango added at the last minute gives this dish a really distinct edge.

Serves 4 to 6

2 tablespoons peanut oil

3 tablespoons curry paste (see below)

1 tablespoon Thai fish sauce

2 tablespoons grated palm sugar *or* raw sugar

1 stalk lemon grass, peeled and finely sliced (thick end only)

1 teaspoon turmeric

1³/4 cups coconut milk

1 lb new potatoes, boiled in skins until tender, then halved

1 teaspoon nigella seeds *or* black mustard seeds

1 lb raw mussels in their shells

¹/3 to ¹/2 lb cockles *or* clams, soaked in water for an hour to remove grit

6 kaffir lime leaves, halved

1 green chile, finely sliced

¹/2 ripe mango, peeled and diced

curry leaves, cilantro, *or* sliced green onions for garnish

Heat oil in a deep saucepan until almost smoking. Add curry paste and gently fry for 1 minute, stirring well. Add Thai fish sauce, sugar, lemon grass, and turmeric and simmer rapidly for a minute, stirring continually. Stir in coconut milk, potatoes, and nigella seeds and bring back to the boil. Add mussels, cockles, and kaffir lime leaves and cover the pan. Bring back to a boil and simmer until shellfish open, then cook another 30 seconds. Stir in chile and mango and spoon into a bowl. Scatter garnish on top. Serve with plain rice.

Curry paste

4 green chiles

2 thumbs fresh ginger, peeled and grated

1 heaped teaspoon turmeric

6 shallots, peeled and sliced

10 cloves garlic, peeled

1 teaspoon ground mace

1 teaspoon salt

1 tablespoon light cooking oil

¹/2 cup plus 1 tablespoon water

Place all ingredients in a food processor and puree to a fine paste.

poultry

Two of my all-time favorite dishes would have to be lemon-roasted chicken with peas and spinach, and duck coconut curry. However, both birds lend themselves to a huge array of other dishes, and both are very versatile, especially chicken. You can usually replace chicken in a recipe with guinea fowl, and duck can be replaced with goose (although much harder to get hold of and also much bigger). Guinea fowl are beautiful birds, shaped much like a soccer ball with grey feathers and black spots. The meat is tasty and tender, although the meat carries less fat than chicken, so it will dry out if overcooked. Ostrich has made some inroads into poultry sections in gourmet markets, and it is also worth trying at home if you can find it. It has a flavor that is unique, full flavored and very tasty so long as it's not overcooked. The meat is healthy and definitely worth searching for to add a spark to a dinner party. I always choose to cook organic or "free-range and hormone-free" birds—the flavor is better, and the bird has had a happier life! A word of warning on chicken: it can become very dry if overcooked, so keep an eye on it.

Chicken, spiced quince, and hummus burger

I like to use boned chicken leg or thigh for this, as the flavor is better and the meat more juicy than a breast. If quinces aren't available, use poached pears instead.

Serves 2

2 boned chicken legs *or* 4 thighs

salt and freshly ground black pepper

olive oil for frying

2 naan breads, 4 inches across

4 tablespoons hummus

1 handful mâche *or* similar greens

$^1/_2$ spiced poached quince (recipe on page 188), sliced

Season chicken well and cook in a frying pan (or on a barbecue) in a little oil, skin side down, until golden brown. Turn over and cook with a lid on (if possible) until cooked through—about 6 to 8 minutes altogether.

Warm naan in the oven or on the gentlest part of the barbecue and split them open, but keep one edge intact. Divide the hummus between the naan, add some mâche and sliced quince, then tuck the chicken in and press down lightly.

Chicken, mushroom, and spinach pies

You'll need to have deep muffin tins to make these cutest of pies. Otherwise, use regular pie tins. Go through your fridge and use leftovers to fill these pies. They are great served cold for lunches or picnics, but they're also good warm from the oven with fruit chutney.

Makes 6

2 large handfuls mushrooms, thickly sliced

3 tablespoons sesame *or* olive oil

3 tablespoons soy sauce

3 tablespoons water

1 lb cold roast chicken, cut into $^1/_2$-inch chunks

$4^1/_2$ cups spinach, blanched, refreshed, and excess water squeezed out

$^1/_2$ teaspoon salt

2 green onions, sliced

2 puff pastry sheets, thawed

1 egg, beaten

Preheat oven to 450°F. Sauté mushrooms in oil, stirring to prevent sticking, until softened. Add soy sauce and water. Cook over a moderate heat until liquid has evaporated, then transfer to a bowl with chicken. Roughly chop spinach and add to bowl with salt and green onions. Gently mix together.

Cut six circles from pastry, about $^3/_4$ inch larger than large muffin pans, and press into tin. Divide filling between pastry shells, making the center form a peak. Cut out six more pastry circles almost the same size as the tins and brush beaten egg around the outside. Flip over and place on top of filling, pressing edges into the top of the pastry shells. Prick three rows of holes in the top with a fork, brush with more egg, and bake 20 to 25 minutes, until very golden brown.

Chicken, mushroom, and spinach pies

Chicken salad with soba noodles

This chilled salad makes a perfect summer starter for six, or it would make a lunchtime main course for three or four. Soba noodles, usually made from a combination of buckwheat and wheat flours, are a staple ingredient in many Japanese kitchens, served either cold in salads or in noodle soups. Green tea noodles, also Japanese and made from wheat flour and powdered green tea, make a stunning alternative.

Serves 6

1 teaspoon oil	2 pinches of sea salt
salt and freshly ground black pepper	1 thumb fresh ginger, peeled and finely grated
2 chicken breasts, skin on	$1/2$ lb soba noodles, cooked as below
$1/2$ cucumber, halved lengthways and seeded	2 green onions, finely sliced
juice of 1 lemon	12 mint leaves, finely shredded
2 teaspoons superfine sugar	good-quality soy sauce

Preheat oven to 450°F. Lightly oil and season chicken breasts on both sides and brown in a frying pan until golden on both sides. Place in oven and roast 15 minutes or until cooked. Let cool, then peel off skin if you want to—I like to keep it on. While they're cooking, peel cucumber into ribbons with a potato peeler, then mix with lemon juice, sugar, salt, and ginger and refrigerate.

To serve, mix noodles, green onions, and mint. Divide into six piles. Finely slice chicken and lay slices over the top of noodles. Lastly, put a pile of cucumber mixture on top and drizzle with a teaspoon or so of the soy sauce.

How to cook soba noodles

Half fill a deep saucepan with water, add a little salt, and bring to a boil. Drop in all the noodles, leave 30 seconds, then stir well. Bring to a boil, then pour in half a cup of cold water (this "shocks" the noodles). Return to a boil and add another half cup of cold water, then boil again. Test noodles to see if they're ready—they should be a little al dente. Once cooked, drain and refresh under cold running water, then drain again and mix carefully with a few tablespoons of sesame oil to prevent them sticking. Keep in the fridge for no more than 2 days.

Tomatoes stuffed with chicken, mint, peanuts, and cilantro

While shopping for the food for this photo shoot, I came across these oddly colored but sweet-tasting tomatoes in St. John's Wood, London. I like to serve these as a light summer brunch, with lots of crusty bread and salad.

Serves 4

8 medium, ripe tomatoes *or* **4 beefsteak tomatoes**

3 single chicken breasts, skin and bones removed, cut into small pieces

1 red onion, peeled and finely sliced

2 tablespoons sesame oil

2 teaspoons Thai fish sauce *or* **1 teaspoon salt**

1 cup loosely packed mint leaves

6 green onions, finely sliced

$^1/_2$ cup lightly toasted peanuts, roughly chopped

3 tablespoons lemon juice

$^1/_4$ cup extra virgin olive oil

$^1/_2$ cup cilantro leaves

freshly ground black pepper

Preheat oven to 325°F. Sit tomatoes on a cutting board, stem side down, and cut the top off, about $^1/_4$ inch deep. Finely dice the top. Scoop inside seeds out with a small teaspoon and push these through a sieve to extract juice or simply discard them if you don't want to be bothered—and on a hot day even I might be pushed to do this!

Fry chicken and onion in sesame oil over a moderate heat until almost cooked. Remove from heat and add diced tomato tops, Thai fish sauce, mint, half the green onions, and peanuts. Mix well, then spoon mixture back inside tomatoes.

Lightly oil a roasting dish and sit tomatoes in, cut sides facing up. Bake for 15 minutes, at which point the skins should almost be bursting, but not quite. Remove from oven and carefully place on a plate. Mix any tomato juices with lemon juice and olive oil and spoon over the tomatoes. Scatter the cilantro and the remaining green onions on the tomatoes and grind on some pepper.

Chicken, parsnips, and mushrooms in a pot

This pays homage to the classic French dish pot-au-feu. I like to use mixed mushrooms (shiitake, button, chestnut, and oyster), but regular mushrooms work just as well. If you don't have a deep saucepan or casserole dish large enough to hold a whole bird, you can use chicken pieces and adjust the cooking time. I like to serve the leftover broth as a soup, adding cooked macaroni and chile to spice it up—it's delicious and will keep for two days in the fridge.

Serves 4 to 6

3 tablespoons olive oil

2 leeks, washed and thickly sliced

2 parsnips, peeled and cut into chunks

4 bay leaves

8 cloves garlic, unpeeled

12 shallots, peeled

1 small handful thyme (on the stem)

$1/3$ to $1/2$ lb assorted mushrooms, cleaned

1 large ($2^1/2$-lb) chicken, trussed and rubbed with

   1 teaspoon salt

salt and freshly ground black pepper

Heat oil in a large deep saucepan or casserole dish (one with a tight-fitting lid that will be able to hold a whole bird) on the stove. Fry leeks, parsnips, bay leaves, garlic, and shallots until they begin to turn golden. Add thyme and mushrooms and fry for another minute.

Place chicken on top of vegetables and pour in enough boiling water to just about cover the bird. Bring to a boil, then turn to a simmer, cover, and poach 60 to 90 minutes. Alternatively, place in an oven preheated to 350°F and cook for 90 minutes. The chicken is cooked when the meat on the thigh is no longer pink—test with a skewer or a small knife. Add a little salt and pepper to taste, then allow to sit in the broth for 15 minutes, off the heat.

Remove chicken to a serving plate and scoop out vegetables with a slotted spoon. Cut up chicken and serve it with vegetables and broth for sauce.

Pomegranate molasses chicken and kumara

Pomegranate molasses is a wonderful thing to have in the kitchen—it has the tang of tamarind and the sweetness of a light honey. It's available from special delis, Turkish and Middle-Eastern markets, and some Asian food shops. If you can't find it, use equal parts maple syrup or honey and tamarind paste instead. This recipe also works well with a very small turkey. It can be eaten hot or cold.

Serves 4

1 large (about 3-lb) chicken

2 teaspoons salt

1 onion, peeled and quartered

4 cloves garlic, unpeeled and crushed

1 small handful mixed herbs (thyme, sage, rosemary, and tarragon)

$1/3$ cup extra virgin olive oil

$1^1/4$ to $1^2/3$ lb orange kumara *or* sweet potatoes, scrubbed and cut into $1^1/4$-inch chunks

Kerry Fox's chicken and barley dinner

My partner, Michael, and I lived in London with New Zealand actress Kerry Fox for over seven years. In fact, her son Eric Linklater was born in our home. We used to take turns at cooking, and this recipe is based on one of Kerry's favorite dishes.

Serves 4

3 tablespoons olive oil *or* 3 tablespoons butter

3/4 cup pearl barley, boiled in plenty of lightly salted water for 15 minutes, then drained

1 large leek, washed and sliced into 1/2-inch rings

2 red onions, thickly sliced

1 medium carrot, peeled and thinly sliced

6 cloves garlic, peeled and halved

1 large handful mixed fresh herbs (rosemary, sage, oregano, thyme, tarragon, basil), roughly chopped

salt and freshly ground black pepper

6 chicken legs (the thigh and drumstick)

about 1 3/4 cups boiling chicken *or* vegetable stock *or* water

Preheat oven to 350°F. Grease a ceramic or roasting dish with olive oil or butter. Place barley in dish and scatter over leek, onions, carrot, garlic, herbs, and salt and pepper.

Cut chicken legs in two at the knee joint. Place on top of vegetables, trying not to overlap. Pour on the boiling stock, which ideally should cover the barley by 1/2 inch—add a little more if necessary. Cover dish with foil and bake 30 minutes in the middle of the oven. Remove the cover and continue baking until chicken is cooked (juices run clear), about 25 minutes. Place under broiler to brown chicken lightly, then serve.

2 teaspoons five spice

1 teaspoon cumin seeds

1 teaspoon fennel seeds

4 teaspoons sesame seeds

1 teaspoon chile flakes *or* chopped fresh red chile

1/4 cup pomegranate molasses

Preheat oven to 525°F. Rinse inside of chicken and dust with 2 teaspoons salt. Stuff cavity with onion, garlic, and herbs, then place chicken, breast side down, in a preheated lightly oiled roasting dish.

Brush chicken with a little more oil, sprinkle with salt and pepper, add 1 cup of boiling water to the dish, and roast for 15 minutes.

Meanwhile, place kumara in a deep saucepan and cover with water. Boil 10 minutes, then drain.

Place remaining oil in a small pan and add spices, seeds, and chile. Fry over a moderate heat until the seeds begin to pop, then remove from heat.

Combine the spicy oil with the kumara and 1 teaspoon salt and place around chicken in the dish, turning chicken over so that the breast now faces upwards. Brush skin with molasses, turn the oven down to 350°F, and continue roasting until chicken and kumara are cooked—about 45 minutes. If the skin begins to burn, cover the bird with foil.

Steamed herb and garlic chicken wrapped in leaves

This recipe is just a starting block—it's the technique that's important; the flavors are really up to you. You can replace the olive oil with Austrian roasted pumpkin seed oil, add some ginger to the marinade, or just use cilantro as the herb . . . I serve this with a mixed-leaf salad tossed with olives, capers, and roasted hazelnuts.

Serves 2

2 chicken breasts, skin removed

1 clove garlic, peeled and finely chopped

1 heaped tablespoon finely chopped fresh herbs (rosemary, thyme, oregano, basil, etc.)

$1/2$ teaspoon Spanish sweet smoked paprika (also called pimentón dulce)

1 teaspoon finely grated mandarin zest *or* orange zest

1 teaspoon coarse sea salt

few grinds black pepper

1 tablespoon extra virgin olive oil

1 onion, quartered

1 bay leaf

2 to 4 large leaves to wrap the chicken in (I used Savoy cabbage leaves, blanched in salted boiling water until soft, but you could use chard, Swiss chard, or vine leaves)

Lay breasts on a cutting board and use a sharp knife to cut two slashes in the skin side of the flesh to a depth of $1/4$ inch. Combine garlic, herbs, paprika, mandarin zest, salt, pepper, and oil and rub into chicken, especially into the slashes. Cover with plastic wrap and marinate in the fridge for 1 to 4 hours.

An hour before serving, take chicken from the fridge, then 30 minutes later bring half a deep saucepan of water to a boil with onion, bay leaf, and a little sea salt added. Place a steamer on top. Put a plate in the steamer that is just large enough to fit, with at least a $1/4$-inch gap around the outside. Place a lid on.

Lay leaves flat on a work surface, place a chicken breast in the center, and wrap leaf tightly around it. Turn chicken over so that the folded-in bits are on the bottom. Place in the steamer, cover, and cook over a rapid boil for 10 to 15 minutes, depending on the size of the chicken. To test if chicken is cooked, remove it and gently cut through the thickest end—the juices should run clear.

Chicken wings with spicy chorizo mash

Chicken wings have that wonderful gelatinous texture when cooked slowly. The chorizo mash was inspired by a visit to the beautiful Spanish town of Cárceres in 2002, where I was served a cold purée with bread—much like you would serve hummus.

Serves 6 as a snack

2 lb chicken wings

1 (14-oz) can peeled tomatoes in juice, chopped, *or* fresh tomatoes

1 red chile, sliced

2 tablespoons sesame seeds

2 tablespoons roasted sesame oil

2 tablespoons golden syrup *or* honey

1 heaping teaspoon salt

6 cloves garlic, peeled and crushed

2^1/2 lb boiling potatoes, peeled and cut into large chunks

^{1}/3 to ^{1}/2 lb chorizo

2 tablespoons olive oil

Mix chicken wings with chopped tomatoes, chile, sesame seeds, oil, golden syrup, salt, and three-quarters of the garlic. Marinate in the fridge for 2 to 12 hours.

An hour before you want to eat, turn oven to 400°F. Line a roasting tray with foil or parchment paper (it'll make cleaning it easier) and add wings, in one layer; pour on ^{1}/2 cup marinade and discard the rest. Bake 45 to 50 minutes, tossing every 15 minutes, until they begin to caramelize and the meat has become firm and white.

Meanwhile, cook potatoes in salted water, then drain. Peel casings off chorizo and roughly chop the meat. Heat a heavy frying pan and add oil, then chorizo. Cook a few minutes over a moderate heat, breaking the chorizo up with a wooden spoon as it cooks to produce a crumbly mixture. Add remaining garlic and cook another minute. Return potatoes to the pan they were cooked in, pour chorizo mixture on top, and mash together. Season to taste.

To serve, spoon the mash onto a plate and top with wings and their cooking juices.

Whiskey-crumbed turkey breast with bean, mango, and peanut salad

This is a totally nonconformist turkey meal—Austrian turkey schnitzel meets Southeast Asia with a bit of whiskey thrown in for good measure. I find the whiskey adds a really subtle flavor to the bird and have often used rum to dip pork chops in before crumbing; you may find it unnecessary—it's up to you. The crunch of the crumbs is important, so make your own from stale white or sourdough bread and avoid those fine premade crumbs.

Serves 6

2 to 2¹/₂ lb turkey schnitzels (skinless, boneless breasts, pounded to a ³/₄-inch thickness)

salt and freshly ground black pepper

¹/₃ to ¹/₂ cup flour

1 egg

3 tablespoons whiskey *or* milk *or* cream

2 cups fresh breadcrumbs

1 cup (2 sticks) butter *or* ¹/₂ cup olive oil

¹/₂ cup lime juice

2 teaspoons Thai fish sauce

1 tablespoon grated palm sugar *or* brown sugar

1 medium-heat chile, finely chopped

1 large mango, peeled and flesh diced

1 bunch cilantro, leaves picked

¹/₂ bunch mint, leaves picked and large ones halved

¹/₂ cup toasted peanuts, roughly chopped

1 cup (about ¹/₃ lb) green beans, blanched and refreshed

Season turkey with salt and pepper and dust with flour. Beat egg with whiskey. One by one dip turkey schnitzels into egg mixture, then coat with crumbs, pressing crumbs firmly into both sides.

Heat a frying pan (you may need to cook this in batches) and add butter or oil. When it stops sizzling, add schnitzels and cook 2 to 3 minutes each side over moderate heat until golden. To test if they're cooked, carefully slice schnitzels open with a sharp knife—the flesh should be white but still a little juicy. (If you're cooking for more than six, it may be easier to seal the schnitzels in a pan, then bake on a tray in the oven at 350°F.)

While they're cooking, mix lime juice, Thai fish sauce, sugar, and chile together. Toss this dressing with mango, cilantro, mint, peanuts, and beans.

To serve, place hot schnitzels on plates and top with salad.

Pan-fried ostrich and wild mushrooms on pumpkin polenta

Ostrich, and the Australian emu for that matter, are both tasty birds, but because they're so lean, they shouldn't be cooked beyond medium in case they dry out. You could also use turkey breast for this recipe if you can't find ostrich in your area. You will need to cook it through, but be careful not to overcook it for the same reason. I like to use dried mushrooms for this recipe as you get some lovely flavor from the soaking liquid. You can, of course, use fresh mushrooms, in which case use a light vegetable stock to make the polenta.

Serves 2

2 (3-oz) ostrich steaks *or* turkey breasts

salt and freshly ground black pepper

$1/2$ cup assorted dried wild mushrooms *or* 1 cup fresh mushrooms

2 tablespoons olive oil

$1/4$ lb pumpkin, peeled and cut into $1/2$-inch chunks

2 cloves garlic, peeled and chopped

$1/4$ cup (4 tablespoons) butter

1 small leek, washed and finely sliced

$1/2$ cup instant polenta

Lightly season ostrich with salt and pepper. Soak dried mushrooms in $2^1/2$ cups warm water for 30 minutes, then drain (check no grit is clinging to them). Save the strained liquid for the polenta. Heat a frying pan (one with a lid) and add half the oil and the pumpkin. Cook over gentle heat for 2 minutes, tossing carefully, until pumpkin begins to color. Mix in garlic, then cover and continue cooking, stirring occasionally, until pumpkin is tender. Remove pumpkin to a small bowl and wipe out the pan.

Put the pan back on the heat and add remaining oil. Add ostrich steaks and cook $1^1/2$ minutes, then turn over. If your steaks are $1/2$ inch thick, you'll need to cook them for just another minute to have them medium-rare. Remove from pan and place on a plate, covered, in a low-temperature oven to keep warm.

Don't wipe the pan, just add half the butter and, when it stops foaming, add mushrooms and sauté until they're cooked, adding a little salt at the end. Place on top of the ostrich in the oven.

Again, don't wipe the pan but add remaining butter and leek and sauté until wilted, then add 2 cups of the mushroom soaking liquid and bring to a boil. Turn to a simmer and sprinkle polenta in, whisking gently to prevent lumps forming, then bring to a gentle boil and stir for a minute. Add pumpkin, check seasoning, and simmer another minute, stirring continually.

Just as you're about to serve, pour any juices that have come from the ostrich into the polenta and mix in. Dollop half the polenta onto each plate and place the ostrich and mushrooms on top.

Duck, ginger, star anise, and coconut stew

This stew is very rich and hearty, and the depth of flavor is enormous. Star anise are seed pods from a tree native to southern China—if you can't find them replace with one flaked cinnamon stick. You can also make this using chicken, which will take about 40 minutes less cooking time.

Serves 6

1 medium duck

2 red onions, peeled and thickly sliced

1 medium leek, cut into $1/2$-inch rings and washed well

1 carrot, peeled and cut into $1/2$-inch cubes

3 cloves garlic, peeled and roughly chopped

$1/3$ cup coarsely grated fresh ginger

6 whole star anise

1 bay leaf

1 teaspoon salt

1 (13.5-oz) can unsweetened coconut milk

1 cup water *or* chicken stock

fresh cilantro to serve

Preheat oven to 350°F. Cut duck into two legs and two breasts, then cut each piece in half again.

Heat a heavy frying pan and brown meat all over without adding any oil. The duck should be fatty enough so it won't need any. Brown only as many pieces as will fit in comfortably at one time. Remove pieces to a plate when they're ready.

Keeping rendered fat in the frying pan, add onions and leek and fry on a high heat, stirring often, until onions begin to color. Put them into the bottom of a large casserole dish with carrot, garlic, ginger, star anise, and bay leaf. Lay duck on top and sprinkle with salt. In the same frying pan, bring coconut milk and water to a boil, then pour over the duck. (If liquid doesn't cover meat, add more hot water.)

Cover the dish and cook 2 hours, then remove lid and cook another 20 minutes. Serve this with fragrant rice topped with lots of fresh cilantro.

Roast duck red curry

Roast duck red curry

The technique of frying the curry paste in coconut oil, made from coconut milk, is an authentic Thai method. The extra curry paste can be kept in the fridge for up to a week or frozen for up to three months. A 3 1/2-lb duck will take about 90 minutes to cook at 350°F. Or to save time, you could buy a precooked duck from an Asian market (which will be delicious) or use a rotisserie chicken from your local shop, if you're lucky to have such a thing. Serve with steamed rice and store-bought or homemade Indian mango chutney.

Serves 4

3 1/3 cups coconut milk

1 to 2 tablespoons curry paste (see below)

1 tablespoon Thai fish sauce

1 heaped tablespoon grated palm sugar *or* raw sugar

2 tablespoons tomato paste

4 kaffir lime leaves

2 red chiles, halved and seeded

1 1/2 cups (1/2 lb) green beans, trimmed

1/2 roast duck, cut into pieces, either on or off the bone

1 small handful Thai basil leaves *or* regular basil

1 small handful cilantro leaves

In a medium-sized pan, bring 1 1/2 cups of the coconut milk to a boil over medium heat, then simmer 4 to 5 minutes until it separates, stirring constantly to ensure it does not scorch. (The nonfat part of the milk will evaporate, leaving the coconut oil.) Add curry paste and fry, stirring constantly, 1 to 2 minutes or until its color deepens and it becomes fragrant.

Add Thai fish sauce, palm sugar, tomato paste, and kaffir lime leaves and simmer for another minute. Stir in remaining coconut milk and chiles and bring to a boil. Add beans and duck, return to a boil, and cover and simmer 5 minutes to warm through. Stir in basil and sprinkle cilantro on top.

Curry paste

4 red chiles, green stems removed

10 shallots *or* 1 large red onion, peeled

8 cloves garlic, peeled

1 thumb galangal, peeled and roughly chopped

2 stalks lemon grass, peeled and finely sliced (thick end only)

3 cilantro roots, washed and finely chopped (optional)

1 teaspoon lime zest

1 teaspoon white peppercorns, ground

2 teaspoons cilantro seeds, toasted in a pan until golden, then crushed

1/2 teaspoon ground cloves

1 teaspoon salt

1/2 cup plus 1 tablespoon water

2 tablespoons light cooking oil

Place all ingredients in a blender or food processor and process to a fine paste.

meat

Although I've eulogized about the joys of vegetables and fish, I have to admit that I occasionally have an enormous hankering for meat, especially meat with fat such as pork belly, mutton, suckling pig, or roast lamb. I'm not really a beef eater, but when I crave a steak I really have to have something like a grilled Longhorn porterhouse. Venison is great because you can almost taste the heather if it's wild and farmed venison is a healthy, lean, delicious, and tender beast. If you haven't tried New Zealand lamb then you must seek it out—it's grass fed, free ranging, and it comes from the most beautiful country—not that I'm biased. All prime cuts of meat are best cooked quickly to no more than medium. Whereas all the muscley joints need to be stewed or braised—cooked gently over a long period in some liquid—never stew lean prime cuts though, as they contain no fat or gristle and will remain forever dry.

Lamb leg coconut curry with green beans and kumara on herbed rice

This dish is extremely rich—the first spring lambs are sweet, as is the coconut milk. I like this made with almost an excess of chile to cut through this sweetness. While rosemary isn't traditional in a coconut curry, its flavor works perfectly with the rest of the ingredients.

Serves 6

4 whole red chiles, seeds intact

8 cloves garlic, peeled

1 bunch cilantro, roots intact, washed well

1/4 cup finely grated root ginger

1/4 cup fresh rosemary leaves

2 limes, zest and juice

2 1/2 lb boned leg of lamb, excess fat removed, cut into 3/4-inch cubes

3 tablespoons peanut oil

4 medium onions, peeled and finely sliced

2 1/2 cups coconut milk

boiling water, enough to cover meat

about 1 lb peeled kumara *or* sweet potatoes, cut into 3/4-inch cubes

about 1 lb green beans, tops removed

3 tablespoons Thai fish sauce

Purée together chiles, garlic, cilantro, ginger, rosemary, and lime zest and juice to a fine paste. Mix into lamb and let marinate for 1 hour. Heat peanut oil in a large saucepan and fry onions until golden. Add meat and brown it, adding a little extra oil if necessary. Add coconut milk and bring to a boil. Pour on enough boiling water to cover meat by 1 1/4 inches and gently simmer for 1 1/2 hours. After an hour, add the kumara and continue to cook for another 20 to 30 minutes (until kumara is almost cooked). Mix in beans and Thai fish sauce. Check seasoning, adding extra Thai fish sauce or salt if needed.

Herbed rice

I like to serve rice at room temperature with a curry, so once the curry is cooking, get the rice on.

1 white onion, peeled and finely diced

2 tablespoons peanut oil

1 bay leaf

2 cups basmati rice *or* jasmine rice, rinsed

3 3/4 to 4 cups cold water

8 green onions, finely sliced

1 large handful basil, shredded

1 large bunch cilantro, coarsely chopped

Fry onion in oil until golden. Add bay leaf and rice and fry, stirring well, for 1 minute. Add water, stir well, cover, and bring to a boil. Cook on high heat for 1 minute, then turn to a low simmer for 10 minutes. Without removing the lid, turn heat off and leave until curry is ready. To finish, stir in green onions, basil, and half the cilantro. To serve, spoon rice into a bowl, ladle curry on top, and sprinkle with remaining cilantro.

Braised lamb shanks with tamarind and dates

This dish is likely to become one of your favorites. It's simple, tasty, and can be left to look after itself once in the oven—one of the joys of a stew. If you can't get shanks, use boned leg of lamb, trimmed of excess fat and cut into 1¹/₂-inch cubes. Boiled potatoes or couscous is ideal with this.

Serves 6

 6 lamb shanks

 3 tablespoons sesame oil

 3 red onions, peeled and quartered

 12 cloves garlic, peeled

 1¹/₄ cups red wine

 3 carrots, grated

 ²/₃ cup tamarind paste

 4-inch sprig fresh rosemary

 ¹/₂ red chile, sliced into rings, seeds intact

 ¹/₄ cup balsamic vinegar

 ¹/₄ cup soy sauce

 meat *or* vegetable stock, enough to cover lamb

 1¹/₄ cups (about ¹/₂ lb) roughly chopped pitted dates

Preheat oven to 525°F. Place the lamb shanks in a deep-sided casserole dish and roast 20 minutes until browned on all sides. While the lamb is browning, heat oil in a frying pan, add onions and garlic, and sauté 3 minutes. Add red wine and bring to a boil.

When lamb has browned, drain off the fat and place shanks back into the casserole dish. Pour wine mixture over lamb. Add all the other ingredients to the casserole dish except dates, ensuring that the meat is covered by the stock (add extra hot water if required). Cover and put in the oven, turning it down to 350°F. Cook 2 hours, then add dates and stir well. Return to the oven and cook another 20 minutes. Season to taste and serve.

Roast lamb neck fillets with minted pea salsa

Lamb neck fillets are much underrated, as they're flavorsome and succulent—and they deserve to be used more. However, if you can't find them, this recipe also works well with grilled chops or roast leg of lamb. I like to serve this salsa all through spring and summer. It is great at a barbecue as it goes well with chicken and snapper, too. Serve this as a main course with boiled potatoes and salad.

Serves 4

 2 tablespoons butter *or* olive oil

 1¹/₄ to 1³/₄ lb lamb neck fillets, trimmed of excess fat and seasoned with salt and freshly ground black pepper

 ¹/₃ to ¹/₂ cup shelled peas (frozen or fresh), cooked and refreshed

 2 green onions, sliced

 1 handful mint leaves

 2¹/₄ tablespoons extra virgin olive oil

 2¹/₄ tablespoons rice wine vinegar *or* cider *or* white wine vinegar

 ¹/₄ teaspoon salt

Preheat oven to 350°F. Heat an ovenproof frying pan on the stove. Add butter and, as soon as it has melted, add the lamb neck fillets. Brown on all sides, then place the pan in the oven and roast 5 to 7 minutes or until fillets are still pink in the middle. Rest meat in a warm place for 5 minutes before serving in ¹/₄-inch slices with the salsa on top.

To make the salsa, place peas, green onions, mint, olive oil, vinegar, and salt in a food processor and pulse for 3 seconds. Scrape down the sides and purée again briefly—the salsa should be a little chunky. Transfer to a bowl and taste for seasoning.

Rosemary and yogurt roast rack of lamb

If you're cooking this on a hot summer's day, then you can barbecue the lamb—just watch that it isn't over the hottest part of the grill, as it may burn before it's cooked. Serve with Pecan and Maple Glazed Yams (page 79), some boiled beans, and fresh tomato salad drizzled with olive oil and lemon juice. You will need four to five racks depending on their size; I allow four cutlets per person.

Serves 6

24 lamb cutlets, on the rack and French trimmed

1 scant cup thick yogurt

1 tablespoon manuka honey *or* any rich honey

2 teaspoons salt

2 tablespoons fresh rosemary, finely chopped

4 cloves garlic, peeled and crushed

oil for cooking

One or two days before serving, trim lamb of fat to the degree you like and score remaining fat in a criss-cross fashion. Combine yogurt, honey, salt, rosemary, and garlic. Rub into lamb, then cover and place in the fridge.

A few hours before the meal, take lamb from the fridge, bring up to room temperature, and wipe off excess marinade.

An hour before the meal, turn oven to 450°F. Heat up a heavy frying pan and add a few teaspoons of oil. Place as many racks as fit comfortably into the pan, fat side down, and cook over a moderate heat to render some of the fat, then turn over and cook another 2 minutes. Transfer to a roasting dish. Place in the oven near the top and roast 15 minutes for medium rare, 20 minutes for medium. Rest in a warm place for at least 10 minutes before serving.

Grilled lamb chops in Worcestershire sauce and beer

What I find really interesting is that Worcestershire sauce (so terribly British and "old-school") contains one of my favorite flavorings: tamarind. Tamarind is something that people find quite unusual, so whenever I tell them that it is used in Worcestershire sauce, they are happy to use it themselves! If you want to be a bit racy, add some chopped garlic and chopped fresh herbs to the marinade. This also works well with pork chops. Serve with potato salad or mashed potatoes and briefly blanched finely shredded cabbage, with mint sauce on the side.

Serves 6

1/4 cup Worcestershire sauce

1²/3 cups draught beer *or* stout

3 lb lamb chops (allow 8 oz per person), trimmed of excess fat if you must, but there's a lot of flavor in that fat!

salt and freshly ground black pepper

Mix sauce and beer together in a nonmetal dish and then add chops. Mix well and allow to marinate for 2 to 12 hours, turning twice.

Drain chops, pat dry, then lightly season. Cook on the barbecue or under a broiler 2 to 3 minutes each side, depending on thickness.

Lamb chops with apple glaze and warm kumara salad

New Zealand has become a country of intriguing food production. Avocado oil and Forage Foods' range of fruit condiments are two of my recent finds. Here I combine them both with lamb and kumara to give me a feel of "back home." Serve this with crusty bread and some shredded iceberg lettuce tossed with lemon juice for a good Sunday brunch.

Serves 4

12 lamb chops

salt and freshly ground black pepper

¹/₃ cup Forage Foods apple glaze *or* **3 tablespoons**
    pure apple juice and 2 tablespoons light honey

¹/₄ cup avocado oil

1 lb kumara *or* **sweet potatoes, scrubbed**

juice of 1 lemon

1 medium red onion, peeled and finely sliced

2 green onions, sliced

Lightly season chops. Mix a quarter of the glaze with 1 tablespoon of the oil and brush over chops. Marinate for an hour or so.

Cut kumara into even-sized chunks. Place in a deep saucepan of cold salted water and boil until just tender, then drain. Mix lemon juice with the red onion and let marinate for 10 minutes, then mix with the cooked kumara. Pour on remaining avocado oil, add some salt and pepper, and gently toss. Cover with foil and keep warm.

The chops are best broiled in the oven or grilled over a barbecue, but, as there is a lot of fructose in the glaze, which gives a delicious caramelized flavor, they can easily burn—just keep an eye on them. I line an oven tray with foil, set the chops on, and broil for 3 to 4 minutes each side, or simply cook over glowing embers on the barbecue.

Once they're cooked, mix green onions into kumara and divide between four plates. Sit chops on top, drizzle with remaining apple glaze, and eat while hot.

Grilled lamb loin with saffron potatoes

This simply prepared lamb teams so well with the potatoes, the saffron, and parmesan, melting into each other and creating a luxurious dish. The potatoes can also be made using cream to replace the wine for a richer winter dish.

Serves 6

2^1/$_2$-lb lamb fillet or short loin, divided into

6 equal-sized portions

2 tablespoons fresh thyme

2 tablespoons extra virgin olive oil

1 teaspoon sea salt

1 teaspoon freshly ground black pepper

Lay a portion of lamb on a work surface and slice horizontally, keeping the lamb in one piece, then butterfly the lamb open and gently flatten out to a thickness of ^{1}/$_3$ inch with a meat hammer. Do the same to remaining five pieces. Mix thyme, oil, salt, and black pepper together and brush over the lamb pieces. Cover and let marinate until potatoes are cooked.

Heat a grill or heavy skillet to smoking. Cook lamb for 30 seconds each side. It will be medium-rare; cook for longer if preferred.

To serve, place lamb on the plate first, then spoon potatoes with their cooking juices on top.

Saffron potatoes

^{1}/$_2$ **scant cup olive oil**

1 large white onion, peeled and finely diced

1 celery stalk, finely diced

1 medium carrot, peeled and finely diced or grated

6 cloves garlic, peeled and sliced

1 generous pinch saffron

2 tablespoons white vinegar

1^1/$_4$ cups moderately sweet white wine

(e.g., dry riesling)

1 to 2 teaspoons sea salt

5 large potatoes, about 2 lb, skins scrubbed

6^1/$_2$ oz finely grated parmesan (about ^{2}/$_3$ cup)

Preheat oven to 400°F. Heat olive oil in a frying pan and add onion, celery, carrot, and garlic and fry until slightly golden, then stir in saffron and vinegar. Boil until the liquid has almost evaporated, then add wine and salt and bring back to a boil. Cut potatoes into ^{1}/$_4$-inch slices and place half in an 8-inch-square ceramic roasting dish. Sprinkle with parmesan and pour half the onion mixture on top. Add remaining potatoes and then the rest of the onion mixture. Cover dish and bake until cooked, about 1 hour; remove lid and cook another 10 minutes.

Sugar-cured lamb loin with fennel, tomato, and basil salad

This salad may seem a little involved, especially as it takes a few days to get the lamb ready, but, once done, it takes just a few minutes to assemble the dish. As it keeps well in the fridge, I think it is better to do twice the amount of lamb shown, and then you'll have it on hand for future quick snacks. Beef fillet can also be cured in the same way.

Serves 6 as a starter

- 1 1/2 lb lamb short loin, trimmed of fat and sinews
- 1 2/3 lb demerara *or* raw sugar
- 1 lb coarse sea salt
- 2 teaspoons dry-toasted fennel seeds, ground
- 4 cloves garlic, finely chopped
- 1/2 cup soy sauce
- 3 tablespoons extra virgin olive oil

To cure the lamb, mix together sugar, sea salt, ground seeds, garlic, soy sauce, and olive oil. Place 1/2 inch of the mixture in the bottom of a nonmetal, rectangular dish just large enough to hold the meat. Place lamb on top and cover with remaining mixture. Seal the dish and refrigerate. Turn the meat the same time the next day, making sure it remains covered with the mixture, then remove from the fridge after 36 hours.

Rinse off excess mixture under cold water, pat dry, then place cured meat on a cake rack in a cool place, away from light—the fridge is a good place. Allow to drain for 2 hours. The lamb is now ready to use and will keep, wrapped in greaseproof paper, then plastic wrap, for 10 to 12 days in the fridge.

Salad

- 1 fennel bulb
- 1 tablespoon lemon juice
- 6 large ripe tomatoes
- 2 large handfuls fresh basil leaves, torn
- 2 tablespoons extra virgin olive oil
- salt and freshly ground black pepper
- sugar-cured lamb, very finely sliced (see left)

Finely slice fennel into rings and toss with lemon juice. Cut tomatoes into 1/2-inch chunks and mix with basil, olive oil, salt, and pepper. Divide tomato salad between six plates and lay finely sliced lamb on top. Drizzle with a little more lemon juice and olive oil.

Lamb and mint couscous

The best things about spring are tender luscious lamb cutlets and new season's garlic. Cooked simply under a very hot broiler and served with a light couscous, they are a treat. A simple green salad also goes well with this.

Serves 4

12 to 16 lamb cutlets

6 tablespoons extra virgin olive oil, divided

salt and freshly ground black pepper

12 cloves garlic, unpeeled

8 to 12 baby beets, washed

1 bay leaf

1 tablespoon fresh rosemary leaves

$3/4$ cup light red wine

2 tablespoons balsamic vinegar

$1^2/3$ cups couscous

$1^1/2$ cups tepid water

$1/4$ cup snipped chives

$1/2$ cup mint leaves, roughly shredded

Preheat oven to 450°F. Brush lamb with 1 tablespoon olive oil, season with salt and pepper, and let sit, covered, at room temperature. Put garlic, beets, bay leaf, rosemary, wine, vinegar, 3 tablespoons olive oil, and some salt and pepper into a small ceramic roasting dish. Cover tightly and roast 45 minutes.

Place couscous in a bowl and pour water over, stir well, then mix in 2 tablespoons olive oil, herbs, 1 heaping teaspoon salt, and some freshly ground black pepper. Leave covered in a warm place for 20 minutes, then mix again—the grains should now be loose and plump. Remove foil from beets and roast another 20 minutes.

Bake cutlets for 2 to 3 minutes on each side depending on thickness, but they will taste best pink. To serve, spoon some couscous into the center of a plate, add some roast beets and garlic on, then set cutlets on top. Drizzle with roasting liquids.

Lamb, kumara, leek, and bean pie

Lamb neck is a much overlooked cut of meat. The following pie is made by first making a stew, which is great eaten as it is with some plain couscous or roasted sweet potatoes, but here I have then taken it a step further, baking it in a pastry shell.

Serves 4

3 tablespoons cooking oil

1 onion, peeled and sliced

1 leek, sliced and washed well to remove grit

4 cloves garlic, peeled and chopped

$1/2$ to $2/3$ lb kumara, sweet potatoes, *or* regular potatoes, peeled and cut into $1/2$-inch cubes

2 lb lamb neck fillet, trimmed of excess sinew, cut into $1^1/4$-inch chunks

1 tablespoon flour

1 teaspoon *each* fresh thyme and rosemary leaves

1 (15-oz) can cooked beans (flageolet, butter beans, *or* chickpeas)

$1^1/4$ cups meat stock

salt and freshly ground black pepper

2 puff pastry sheets, thawed

1 egg, beaten

Lamb with tomato-stuffed peppers

I like the double cooking method (poaching, then roasting) of not-so-lean meats. (See Twice-Cooked Pork and Olives on Pesto Mash, page 159.) This is good served cold the following day, so you could make it a day in advance for a picnic or buffet lunch.

Serves 4

2¹/₂ lb lamb leg, bone in or boned and tied

1 large onion, peeled and quartered

1 bouquet garni

6 cloves garlic, peeled

4-inch stalk rosemary

2 teaspoons salt

1 red onion, peeled and diced

4 red bell peppers, halved lengthways and seeded

8 to 12 smallish tomatoes, halved

¹/₃ cup extra virgin olive oil

3 teaspoons balsamic vinegar

salt and freshly ground black pepper

Place lamb, onion, bouquet garni, 2 cloves of garlic, and rosemary into a saucepan large enough to hold everything comfortably, cover with water, and add 2 teaspoons salt. Bring to a boil and simmer 30 minutes.

Turn the oven to 450°F. Drain cooking liquid from the pan, place everything into a roasting dish, and bake 15 minutes. Meanwhile, place some finely sliced garlic and diced red onion in each pepper half. Add 2 to 3 tomato halves, cut side up, to each one.

Take lamb from the oven, drain off fat, discard vegetables, and turn lamb over. Place peppers in the dish and drizzle everything with olive oil and vinegar. Season with salt and pepper. Turn oven to 325°F and cook the lamb to whatever stage you like (about 15 minutes for medium). You may need to cook the peppers slightly longer. Let lamb rest for at least 30 minutes before carving.

Heat oil in a deep saucepan and fry onion, leek, and garlic until they begin to caramelize, stirring occasionally. Add kumara and cook 1 minute, then transfer to a bowl.

Place saucepan back on the heat and add a little more oil. Add lamb and brown on all sides. Sprinkle flour in and mix, then add leek mixture, herbs, beans, meat stock, and enough water to cover the meat by ³/₄ inch. Bring to a boil, turn to a simmer, and cook, covered, for 90 minutes. Remove lid and keep cooking until most of the liquid has evaporated, stirring occasionally. Check seasoning and cool completely, then place in the fridge to go cold.

Preheat the oven to 375°F. Unfold the puff pastry sheets and place each on a lightly floured baking sheet and brush the pastries all over with beaten egg. Spoon chilled mixture along one half of each pastry, leaving a 1¹/₄-inch border. Fold pastry over filling and seal the edges by pressing with a floured fork. Brush tops with more egg and prick all over with a fork. Bake for 35 to 40 minutes until dark golden brown.

Herb-crumbed calves' liver with garlic roasted acorn squash

Serve this main course with plain mashed potatoes. You can substitute lambs' liver if you prefer, and if you can't find acorn squash, use chunks of zucchini or butternut squash.

Serves 4

6 to 7 slices of 1-day-old, good-quality bread, cut into chunks

1 small handful mixed fresh herbs (oregano, sage, thyme, rosemary, etc.)

1¼ lb calves' liver, trimmed of sinew, cut into ½-inch slices (ideally 4 even-sized slices)

1 cup flour, seasoned with black pepper and 2 teaspoons salt

1 egg, beaten

⅓ cup (5⅓ tablespoons) butter

4 large cloves garlic, peeled and quartered

8 small yellow acorn squash, quartered

⅓ cup sherry vinegar

¼ cup extra virgin olive oil

salt to taste

1 cup baby spinach, washed well

Place bread and herbs in a food processor and pulse to make crumbs. Lightly dust liver with seasoned flour, dip in egg, and coat evenly with breadcrumbs, pressing them on firmly.

Heat half the butter in a saucepan and add garlic. Fry until just golden, then add squash and 2 tablespoons water. Cover the pan and gently cook until tender, about 15 minutes, shaking occasionally. Remove to a warm plate and keep in a low oven.

Add remaining butter to pan. When sizzling, add liver and turn heat to medium. Fry about 1½ minutes each side or until just beyond the pink stage. Place on a warm plate in the oven. Add sherry vinegar and 1 scant teaspoon salt to the pan and simmer, scraping up the bits that have been cooked on, then add olive oil and turn the heat off.

To serve, divide spinach between four plates, add the squash, then the liver. Top with the hot dressing.

Veal chops with vanilla-braised butter beans

Veal, beans, and vanilla . . . sounds odd but tastes good. These beans go well with other, more fatty meat too, especially duck and pork. You will need to start this the day before if you're going to make the bean stew from scratch, or you could use cooked beans to speed it up considerably.

Serves 6

1 cup dried butter beans

3 tablespoons extra virgin olive oil, plus extra for basting

1 cup (2 sticks) butter

3 medium onions, peeled and finely sliced

2 cloves garlic, peeled and chopped

1 vanilla bean, split down the middle

1 bay leaf

2 cups dry white wine

salt and freshly ground black pepper

18 to 24 veal cutlets (depending on size and the hunger of your guests)

4 tomatoes, peeled, seeded, and cut into chunks

2 lb spinach, washed well and thick stems discarded

Place beans in a large deep saucepan and add at least six times their volume in cold water. Leave overnight in a cool place. Next day, bring to a boil, then drain and discard water. Add fresh water to cover them by 4 inches. Bring to a boil and cook until almost tender (test by biting into one). Drain and set aside.

Place oil and half the butter in a pot and place over a moderate heat. When butter begins to sizzle, add onions and garlic and sauté until onions are soft and slightly colored. Add vanilla bean and bay leaf and cook 4 to 5 minutes, stirring occasionally. Return beans to pot. Add wine and enough hot water to barely cover. Bring to a boil, cover pot, and simmer for 20 minutes. Uncover, season with salt and pepper, and cook until liquid has reduced a third.

Season cutlets with salt and pepper and baste with a little olive oil. Cook over a barbecue or under a broiler. Once they're ready (they should be pink and juicy on the inside), take off the heat and keep warm, covered lightly with a little foil.

Heat up a large pan, add the remaining butter, and once it stops sizzling, add tomatoes. Cook over a high heat 1 minute, stirring well. Add spinach and cook, stirring, until it wilts slightly. Season with salt. To serve, place some spinach on a plate, lay three to four chops on top, and spoon beans over the chops.

Veal racks with potato, basil, and horseradish salad

Cook veal racks the same way as lamb racks—slightly pink—and savor the meat that clings to the bones. Fresh horseradish can sometimes be hard to find, but a good brand of prepared horseradish will do the trick if you're stuck.

Serves 4

1 lb new potatoes, washed

1 lemon grass stem, smashed, then cut into 4

2 teaspoons salt

1 medium red onion, finely sliced

2 tablespoons vinegar

1 to 2 teaspoons freshly grated horseradish *or*

   2 teaspoons horseradish from a jar

1/3 cup light olive oil

4 6-cutlet veal racks

salt and freshly ground black pepper

1 handful basil leaves, torn

Preheat oven to 450°F. Place potatoes and lemon grass in a saucepan, cover with cold water, add salt, and boil until tender, about 15 minutes, slightly more for larger ones. Drain in a colander. Meanwhile mix onion with vinegar and horseradish and let marinate 30 minutes.

Just before potatoes are cooked, heat a heavy frying pan, and preheat a roasting dish in the top of the oven. Rub a few teaspoons of oil over veal, season with salt and pepper, and when the pan is hot, add racks and gently brown all over. Transfer to hot roasting dish and roast 10 to 20 minutes, depending on preferred doneness. Turn oven off, cover racks with foil, and keep the oven door ajar.

Cut warm potatoes in half and mix with onions. Add remaining oil, season well, and stir. Just before serving, mix in basil. Divide salad between four plates and place a rack on each one.

Grilled tongue with wasabi salsa verde and potato salad

I can still remember Gran's jellied ox tongue, but I have to admit it's not the fondest of memories. I prefer to grill tongue, serving it warm and juicy with a piquant sauce. Your butcher should be able to sell you sliced, cooked tongue; otherwise you'll have to cook it yourself—follow the How to Cook Tongue recipe opposite.

Serves 6 as a starter

24 cherry tomatoes, off the stem

1 lb baby potatoes

1/2 teaspoon finely grated lemon zest

1/2 cup extra virgin olive oil

1 small red onion, peeled and finely sliced into rings

1/4 cup lemon juice

salt and freshly ground black pepper

1 firmly packed cup chopped mixed "soft" herbs

   (cilantro, parsley, dill, tarragon, mint, etc.)

1 teaspoon wasabi powder *or* paste *or* grain mustard

1 1/4 lb cooked tongue, cut into 2/3-inch-thick pieces

cooking oil for basting

Roast pork belly

This is the first of two versions of how to cook a pork belly. It is perhaps not viewed as one of the healthiest of meats as it's high in fat, but it's definitely one of the tastiest and is great to eat in winter as it's so rich and comforting. Roast pork belly with mashed rutabaga or sweet potato is just so good.

Serves 4

3 teaspoons salt

2 teaspoons sugar

2 lb pork belly (ask the butcher to remove the bones and score the skin by slashing it at ¼-inch intervals)

Turn oven to 350°F. Rub salt and sugar into scored skin as well as the skinless side. Lay the belly on a cake rack, skin side up, and sit the rack in a roasting dish, suspended about 1¹/₂ inches from the base of the dish—you may want to sit it on some dariole molds or muffin tins. Pour a cup of boiling water into the dish, avoiding the belly, and place in the oven. Roast 1 hour, then turn over and roast another 30 minutes.

By now the pork should be cooked. Check by cutting it with a sharp knife an inch or so in from the side—it should be a pale cooked pink and not raw-looking. If it's not done, cook another 20 minutes. Turn back over and place 4 inches from the top of the oven, turn the broiler on, and cook until the skin is crispy.

You can now eat it as it is or let it cool, then slice thickly and grill or barbecue it, brushing with some oyster or hoisin sauce.

Place tomatoes on parchment paper on a baking tray and roast at 450°F until they just begin to pop. Or heat up a frying pan and cook them in a little oil, shaking occasionally until they pop. Set aside.

Cook potatoes in lightly salted water, drain, and slice ¹/₂ inch thick, then combine with lemon zest and 1 tablespoon of the olive oil. Break onion slices into rings and mix with three-quarters of the lemon juice and a little salt and pepper.

To make salsa verde, mix herbs with remaining olive oil, wasabi, and a pinch of salt. Mix well, then mix in remaining lemon juice.

To serve, brush tongue with a little oil and grill or sauté until warmed through. Mix marinated onion with potatoes and divide between six plates. Lay tongue on top, then scatter on tomatoes and drizzle with the salsa verde, or serve it separately in a bowl.

How to cook tongue

Buy a raw pickled or brined ox tongue (or you may want to use several lambs' tongues), place in a bowl of cold water, and leave for 1 hour. Change the water and leave for another hour. Do this once more so the tongue has soaked for a total of 3 hours.

Drain and place in a large pot with 2 large carrots, peeled and halved, 1 onion, peeled and halved, some herbs, 1 to 2 bay leaves, and 1 cup vinegar. Cover with cold water and bring to a boil. Simmer until the skin can be easily peeled back from the flesh (60 to 90 minutes for lambs' tongues, 2 to 2¹/₂ hours for pig and ox tongues).

Let cool in the liquid and peel when cooled. Store in the fridge for up to 5 days.

Pork belly hot-pot with chile, baby beets, morels, and miso

I bought the pork belly for this recipe already roasted from Chinatown because I was lazy. You can cook it yourself (see Roast Pork Belly, page 155). This dish can be made in the morning and thrown in the oven an hour before you want to eat. Miso paste is available from Japanese and health-food stores and some Asian markets.

Serves 6

2 lb roasted pork belly, boneless

18 dried morels *or* other wild mushrooms, soaked in
   1²/₃ cups warm water for 15 minutes

2 thumbs fresh ginger, peeled and finely sliced

2 cloves garlic, peeled and sliced

1 red chile, sliced

18 baby beets, boiled or roasted until cooked, then
   peeled, *or* 1 small can baby beets, drained

1 heaped tablespoon miso paste

1 cup dry sherry

2 tablespoons soy sauce

Preheat oven to 375°F. Cut pork belly into ³/₄-inch cubes. Take morels from soaking water (don't discard) and rinse gently to remove any grit. Place in a ceramic dish with a tight-fitting lid. Add ginger, garlic, chile, and baby beets and scatter on the pork. Mix miso with sherry and soy sauce and pour over pork, then add the strained mushroom water. Cover dish and cook 1 hour. Serve with rice or noodles.

Roast pork belly à la Anna Hansen

The most constantly inspirational chef I have ever worked with is chef Anna Hansen. Anna and I have worked together in three different restaurants in London. We currently consult for PUBLIC restaurant in New York's Nolita district. Her idea of brining pork belly may seem very simple, but it makes a roasted pork belly a thing of beauty—and it tastes so much better. The flavors you add to the brine are up to you. You want the skin scored with a very sharp knife. The closer the lines, the crisper the crackling. This will make a fantastic meal served with Christmas Mince Roast Kumara (see page 90), a simple arugula salad, and homemade apple sauce.

Serves 8 to 10

4 to 5 lb pork belly, bones removed, skin scored as above

³/₄ cup fine table salt

2 tablespoons allspice, coarsely ground

6 star anise, coarsely ground

1 tablespoon fennel seeds, lightly toasted

1 tablespoon chile flakes (optional)

2 thumbs fresh ginger, finely sliced (don't bother peeling them)

You need to store the belly at least 24 hours in the brine—ideally in a fridge, although a cold room away from sun will do. You may have to chop it into two to three pieces to fit your container. Place everything except pork in a large tub and add 3 quarts cold water. Mix to dissolve salt, then add pork and enough cold water to cover (you may need to weigh the pork down to keep it submerged). Leave 24 to 36 hours.

When it's ready to cook, remove belly from the brine and rinse under cold water, then set on a rack in a roasting tray lined with parchment paper or foil (it'll be easier to clean). Roast on the middle shelf at 320°F for 3¹/₂ hours, by which time the skin should be crackling. Turn the oven up to 400°F and cook until the crackling is crisp. Let rest for 20 minutes, covered with some foil to keep it warm.

Pork, ginger, peanut, and vanilla pasties

Vanilla may seem an odd flavor to accompany pork, but it actually works really well. I find small individual pasties the best way to serve this, but you could make one large pie instead. Delicious with yogurt dipping sauce.

Serves 6

2 medium red onions, peeled and finely sliced

2 tablespoons cooking oil

1 thumb fresh ginger, finely grated

$1/4$ cup fresh orange juice

1 vanilla bean

$1^{1}/2$ cups lean pork, finely diced

1 teaspoon salt

1 cup crunchy peanut butter

1 cup chopped cilantro leaves

2 lb flaky pastry *or* prepared pie crust dough

1 egg, lightly beaten

2 tablespoons sesame seeds

Fry onions in oil until caramelized, stirring well to prevent burning. Add ginger and orange juice and cook until juice evaporates. Split vanilla bean down the middle and scrape out seeds with the back of a small knife, then add seeds and pod to the saucepan. Add pork and salt and gently cook 5 minutes, stirring well. Let cool in the saucepan, then stir in peanut butter and cilantro.

Preheat oven to 375°F. On a lightly floured cutting board, roll out pastry to $1/8$ inch thick and cut out six circles, 7 to 8 inches in diameter. Brush beaten egg around outside of pastry. Remove vanilla pod from pork mixture, scraping it between your fingers to remove any filling, then stir well with a spoon, taste for seasoning, and adjust if necessary.

Divide filling between the pastries, placing mounds of it in the center of each one. Fold each one in half, gently pushing out any air and making sure the edges are sealed tightly by pressing with the back of a fork. Lightly brush with beaten egg and sprinkle with sesame seeds.

Bake on a baking sheet for 25 to 35 minutes, until puffy and golden. Serve with yogurt dipping sauce.

Yogurt dipping sauce

$1^{1}/4$ cups thick, Greek-style plain yogurt

$1/2$ cup cilantro leaves

$1/4$ cup chopped mint leaves

2 tablespoons lemon juice

3 tablespoons soy sauce

Simply mix all the ingredients together.

Twice-cooked pork and olives on pesto mash

This takes a bit of time, but the result is worth it—and the mash is a treat in itself.

Serves 6 to 8

3 lb boned and rolled pork shoulder

1 onion, peeled and quartered

2 fresh chiles

2 carrots, peeled and chopped

2 bay leaves

6 sprigs rosemary

$1/_2$ cup vinegar

2 tablespoons salt

1 cup black olives

$3/_4$ cup plump raisins

3 tablespoons golden syrup *or* honey

Place pork, onion, 1 chile (halved), carrots, bay leaves, 2 rosemary sprigs, vinegar, and salt in a saucepan large enough to hold pork. Cover with cold water and bring to a boil. Cover and simmer 90 minutes. Let cool in the liquid, then proceed, or refrigerate for up to 2 days.

Preheat oven to 350°F. Take pork from liquid, strain off 1$2/_3$ cups, and discard the rest. Place pork in a casserole dish large enough to hold it and pour the reserved liquid on top. Tuck remaining rosemary into the pork and add olives, remaining chile (sliced), raisins, and golden syrup. Cover and bake 45 minutes, then remove lid and roast until liquid has become almost a caramel. Remove pork from pot, take off the string, and slice pork about $1/_4$ inch thick. Dollop some mash on the plate, add some sliced pork, then spoon the olive mixture over the top.

Pesto mash

$2^1/_2$ lb potatoes

1 cup (2 sticks) butter

$2/_3$ cup cream

$2/_3$ cup basil pesto

Boil peeled potatoes in salted water until tender. Bring butter and cream to a boil and mix in pesto. Drain potatoes and mash. Stir in warm basil cream. Season to taste.

Marinated pork chops with apricot and almond rice

Most cuts of pork (trim pork being the exception) are a forgiving meat to cook with as there is a good amount of fat present that generally keeps it good and succulent—no matter how much you overcook it. Don't cook pork on too high a heat, but do cook it through—a rare pork chop will have your guests sending it back!

Serves 4

   2 teaspoons ground star anise

   2 thumbs fresh ginger, finely chopped or grated

   2 tablespoons olive oil

   1 tablespoon manuka honey *or* other rich honey

   4 (6^{1}/$_{2}$-oz) pork chops

   salt and freshly ground black pepper

   1 cup basmati rice, rinsed

   12 dried apricots, quartered

   ^{1}/$_{2}$ cup sliced almonds, toasted

   1 lemon, quartered

Combine star anise, ginger, oil, and honey and rub into chops, cover, and marinate in the fridge for 2 to 12 hours.

An hour before you want to serve them, take chops from the fridge to come to room temperature. Season on both sides with salt and pepper and rub marinade into meat a little.

Place rice in a small saucepan (about 1 quart) with a tight-fitting lid. Add 2^{1}/$_{2}$ cups cold water and a few good pinches of salt. Bring to a boil and add apricots and almonds. Turn down heat, cover, and cook on a rolling simmer for 10 minutes. Turn off heat and leave covered for 15 minutes in a warm place to finish cooking.

Meanwhile, grill or barbecue chops about 4 minutes each side until just cooked through. Best way to test this is to cut them near the bone with a sharp knife—the meat should be white, not pink, on the inside.

To serve, gently mix rice to disperse the nuts and apricots, then divide between four plates. Put a chop on top and serve with a wedge of lemon.

Pot-roasted rabbit chops with green onions and olives

I must admit this dish looks like something you'd feed little eaters. To turn it into a big person's meal, cook the legs as well. To get rabbit chops, buy a skinned and prepared rabbit and split it down the middle. Then, using a heavy, sharp knife, cut the rack off each side, leaving you with fore and rear legs and some other bits, including some of the fillet. These can be roasted or slowly braised.

Serves 4 as a small starter

   1 rabbit, prepared as above, to give you 2 racks

   3 tablespoons extra virgin olive oil

   12 to 16 olives (a mixture of black and green works well)

   1 clove garlic, peeled and finely sliced

   1 teaspoon fresh thyme leaves

   1 teaspoon rosemary leaves

   4 green onions, cut into 2-inch lengths

   1 orange; peel ^{1}/$_{2}$ of the skin off and remove any pith

   3 tablespoons sherry *or* Madeira *or* port

   salt and freshly ground black pepper

   3 tablespoons hot water

   2 tablespoons unsalted butter

Rub rabbit racks with a little oil and lightly season. Heat remaining oil in a heavy pan with a tight-fitting lid. Add racks and brown all over. Remove racks and set aside (don't wipe the pan).

Add olives to the pan and cook over a moderate heat until they begin to wrinkle. Add garlic and herbs and cook until herbs are wilted. Add green onions, orange peel, sherry, and a little seasoning.

Return rabbit to pan, add the water, and cover tightly. Turn to a gentle heat and cook 5 minutes, then remove from heat and stand 5 minutes. Remove racks from pan and keep warm, add butter to the pan, and bring sauce back to a boil.

To serve, divide sauce between four warm plates. Slice racks into cutlets and sit these on top of the sauce.

Pot-roasted rabbit chops with green onions and olives

Grilled beef fillet on wok-fried noodles

This marinade not only flavors the meat, but it "cures" it slightly, firming the flesh and changing its texture. You will need to marinate the meat a few days before you need it.

Serves 4

4 tablespoons demerara *or* raw sugar

2 red chiles, finely chopped

1²/₃ lb trimmed beef fillet, excess fat
    and sinew removed

2¹/₂ cups soy sauce

peanut oil for cooking

1 lb dried egg noodles

2 cups (about ²/₃ lb) green beans, trimmed
    and blanched

1 cup cilantro leaves

1 tablespoon ginger, peeled and finely grated

Rub sugar and chiles into fillet and place it in a nonmetal dish that will comfortably hold it. After 1 hour, turning fillet once, pour soy sauce over meat, cover the dish with plastic wrap, and refrigerate. Turn meat by a quarter rotation every 12 hours for 2 days.

Remove meat from marinade. Reserve 2 tablespoons of the marinade and discard the rest. Wipe meat dry with a cloth, then cut it into four equal-sized steaks and brush with peanut oil.

Cook egg noodles following instructions on the packet, then pour through a colander to drain. Refresh under cold water and drain again.

Heat a heavy frying pan or skillet. Place oiled fillet pieces in the pan, cut side toward the heat, and cook over a moderate to high heat for 2¹/₂ to 3 minutes on each side. This will give you a medium-rare fillet.

Heat a wok to smoking point and add 2 tablespoons peanut oil, swirl it around the wok, and add beans. Toss them lightly to give a little color, then remove with a slotted spoon. Add another tablespoon peanut oil, then add noodles and don't stir for 30 seconds. Using two large spoons or tongs, start tossing noodles gently, trying to brown them a little as well. Return beans to the wok, add 2 tablespoons of marinade, the cilantro, and ginger, and toss together. Divide noodles between four plates and place a piece of grilled beef on each.

Beef spare ribs with black beans, red onions, and soy

Spare ribs are a really good summer picnic affair, but they also make a great winter dish, so long as you have a big napkin to wear.

Serves 2

- $^1/_2$ scant cup maple syrup *or* golden syrup *or* honey
- 2 tablespoons salted Chinese black beans, rinsed briefly
- 2 thumbs fresh ginger, peeled and chopped
- about 1 lb beef spare ribs
- 2 red onions, peeled and sliced
- 6 cloves garlic, peeled and crushed
- $^1/_2$ cup soy sauce
- 1 cup boiling water

Combine maple syrup, black beans, and ginger in a bowl and rub all over ribs. Cover tightly with plastic wrap and refrigerate for 4 to 12 hours, tossing once or twice to make sure they marinate evenly.

Preheat oven to 400°F. Place ribs and marinade into a roasting dish just large enough to hold them. Add onions, garlic, soy sauce, and water and cover tightly. Bake 50 minutes, then remove cover and turn the ribs over. Cook another 45 to 60 minutes, basting with cooking juices, until ribs are dark brown and caramelized and the meat is beginning to come off the bones.

Venison with creamy mushroom and horseradish sauce

This sauce is one of the simplest you can make—in fact, I first learned it in Melbourne as an apprentice chef back in 1982. It isn't exactly healthy, but it's really delicious. Use venison fillet, short loin, or Denver leg fillets and serve with mashed potatoes.

Serves 4

1²/₃ lb venison (see above)

2 teaspoons freshly ground black pepper

1 teaspoon salt

2 tablespoons cooking oil

4 tablespoons butter

1 red onion, peeled and finely sliced

¹/₃ to ¹/₂ cup mushrooms, finely sliced

2 teaspoons freshly grated horseradish *or* horseradish from a jar

2 teaspoons grain mustard

1 cup heavy cream

¹/₂ cup chopped chives

Pat venison with paper towels to absorb excess blood, then place on a plate, sprinkle with half the pepper and salt, and rub it in. Turn fillets over and rub in remaining seasoning. Let sit for 10 minutes, then brush with oil.

Heat a frying pan until it just begins to smoke, then lay in venison and press down firmly. Cook over a moderate to high heat for 2 minutes without touching, then turn over and continue cooking. As a general rule, to cook to rare will take about 1 to 2 minutes more, medium 4 to 5 minutes. (If you like your venison well done, it's better to slice each fillet in half before cooking to prevent them from burning and drying out.) Place cooked venison on a plate and keep in a warm place while you make the sauce.

Add butter to the pan (don't wash the pan first) and fry until it begins to foam, then add onion and fry until softened. Add mushrooms and sauté until they begin to color, then stir in horseradish, mustard, and cream. Bring to a boil and cook until reduced to a thick consistency. By now some juices will have run from the meat, so pour these off the plate into the pan as well. Taste for seasoning and stir in chives at the last minute, then spoon over venison.

Venison dumpling stew with chorizo

Farmed deer have become a recognizable animal in the New Zealand landscape; they are the descendants of deer that British settlers took to New Zealand to hunt for sport. However, these wild animals inevitably broke free and bred and bred and bred! So began the rapid destruction of our native bush. So, as with most things wild, man decided to tame them and began a culling and breeding process, resulting in numerous farms all over the country, where the meat is now marketed as Cervena. However (enough of the history lesson), you could use any venison meat for this, wherever it comes from. Dried wood ear mushrooms (or cloud ear mushrooms) are sold in Asian food shops. Dried shiitake mushrooms can be used instead.

Serves 4

1¹/4 lb ground venison (use haunch or leg; don't use expensive fillet)

¹/2 teaspoon salt

¹/2 teaspoon cracked pepper

2 tablespoons flour

¹/4 cup olive oil

2 onions, peeled and sliced

1 large carrot, peeled and cut into chunks

12 cloves garlic, unpeeled

1 tablespoon dried oregano

¹/3 lb cooking chorizo, cut into ¹/4-inch slices

2 cups light meat stock

¹/4 cup soy sauce

dried wood ear mushrooms, soaked in 2 cups warm water for
   30 minutes

1¹/4 lb large potatoes, cut into wedges

Mix venison, salt, and pepper and roll into 12 equal-sized balls. Roll in flour. Heat 3 tablespoons of the oil in a saucepan and fry onions, carrot, garlic, and oregano until colored. Remove from pan. Add remaining oil and brown the meatballs and chorizo—you may want to do this in two batches. Return vegetables to the pan and add stock, soy sauce, and enough strained mushroom soaking water to just cover the meatballs. If there is not enough liquid, just add some boiling water. Cut mushrooms into fat strips and add to the pan with potatoes, then bring to a simmer. Cover and simmer on the stove or bake in the oven at 350°F for 45 minutes, or until potatoes are cooked.

cookies, cakes, and tarts

All these treats are great wheeled out theatrically on a tea trolley or simply placed on the table alongside afternoon tea and coffee. How nice to offer someone a homemade cookie rather than something from a package. Some of my earliest childhood memories are of jars full of cookies and tins jammed full with assorted cakes, all made by my paternal grandmother, Molly Gordon. I remember as a kid eating Afghan cookie dough (I don't know why they're called Afghans, as they contain cocoa, cornflakes, butter, and sugar)—it was as delicious as the final baked cookies! Get the kids into baking, or get into it yourself—it's really satisfying and smells so good. Some of these recipes also make for good desserts. See what grabs your fancy.

Chocolate, ginger, macadamia, and chile cookies

Chocolate and ginger go well together; ginger and chile go well together—do chile and chocolate? I think they can.

Makes 30

$1/2$ **cup (1 stick) unsalted butter**

$1/2$ **cup plus 1 tablespoon demerara *or* raw sugar**

1 egg

$1/2$ **fresh red chile, finely sliced**

1 scant cup flour

1 teaspoon cornstarch

$1/2$ **teaspoon baking soda**

pinch salt

$3 1/2$ **oz chocolate, in chunks**

$1/2$ **cup macadamia nuts, halved**

$1/4$ **cup candied ginger, chopped**

Preheat oven to 350°F. Line two baking trays with parchment paper. Blend butter, sugar, egg, and chile in a food processor until creamy. Add flour, cornstarch, baking soda, and salt and mix to form a dough. Transfer the dough to a bowl and stir in chocolate, nuts, and half the ginger. Divide the mixture into 30 even-sized pieces and place 15 pieces of dough on each tray, leaving room for spreading. Sprinkle remaining ginger over cookies, then bake until golden brown, about 20 minutes. As you take the trays from the oven, bang them on a counter to release air. Cool cookies on the trays. Store in an airtight container for up to 2 weeks.

Lime, clove, and macadamia cookies

Lime and clove, for some reason, work really well together; it's as if they hit the higher notes in your mouth. I'm currently on a macadamia fad, but if you're not, then replace them with any mild nut you prefer—almonds and peanuts are good.

Makes 24

1 cup (2 sticks) unsalted butter, at room temperature

$^1/_2$ cup confectioners' sugar

2 teaspoons finely grated lime zest

1 teaspoon freshly ground cloves

1 cup flour

$^3/_4$ cup cornstarch

$^1/_2$ teaspoon baking powder

$^3/_4$ cup macadamia nuts, roughly chopped

Preheat oven to 350°F. Line two baking sheets with parchment paper. Cream butter, confectioners' sugar, zest, and cloves until pale. Sift flour, cornstarch, and baking powder and mix into butter, then stir in nuts. Divide mixture into 24 balls and place on baking sheets, leaving 4 inches between each one.

Lightly press mixture down with your thumb, then bake for 16 to 20 minutes, until they go just a little golden. Cool on the tray for 2 minutes, then transfer to a cake rack with a metal spatula and let cool. Store in an airtight container for up to a week.

Spiced fennel, lemon, and sesame cookies

Slightly savory and just a little sweet, these cookies provide a strangely delicious addition to the cookie jar.

Makes about 20

- 1 cup (2 sticks) unsalted butter, at room temperature
- 1 teaspoon finely grated lemon zest
- 3/4 cup confectioners' sugar
- 1 cup flour
- 1/2 cup cornstarch
- 1/4 cup polenta
- 1/4 teaspoon paprika
- 1/2 teaspoon baking powder
- 1 teaspoon ground fennel seeds
- 3 teaspoons sesame seeds, toasted
- 1/4 cup firmly packed brown sugar

Preheat oven to 350°F. Line two baking sheets with parchment paper. Cream butter with lemon zest and confectioners' sugar. Sift in flour, cornstarch, polenta, paprika, and baking powder. Add seeds and mix to combine. Roll walnut-sized pieces into balls. Roll each ball in brown sugar to lightly coat, then place 1 1/2 inches apart on the baking sheet and press down lightly with your fingers. Bake 15 to 20 minutes until golden. Cool on the tray. Store in an airtight container for up to 2 weeks.

Coffee pistachio chocolate truffles

These rich and easy-to-make truffles make a perfect end to a meal. If you don't drink coffee, add a liqueur instead.

Makes about 32

- 12 oz dark chocolate
- 1/2 cup very strong espresso, chilled
- 1/2 cup cream, straight from the fridge
- 2 cups shelled pistachio nuts, lightly toasted and roughly chopped

Melt chocolate in a metal bowl over a pot of simmering water, then remove from the heat. Combine coffee and cream and pour over chocolate, mixing well. Mix in half the nuts, then let cool in the refrigerator until mixture becomes quite firm, stirring once or twice as it cools. Take large marble-sized lumps and roll in remaining nuts, making sure they don't look too perfect or smooth. These will keep in the refrigerator for up to one month.

Changa nut shortbread

I consult for a beautiful restaurant in Istanbul called changa, just off the noisy Taksim Square. The most commonly used nuts in Turkey are hazel and pistachio, so it seems appropriate that I use them both here. These cookies are great served with espresso or mint tea.

Makes 60

1 cup (2 sticks) unsalted butter

1 cup demerara *or* raw sugar

1 egg

$^1/_3$ cup brandy

$^1/_2$ cup pistachios, ground

$^3/_4$ cup hazelnuts, toasted and ground

$3^1/_3$ cups flour, sifted

2 teaspoons baking powder

$^1/_2$ teaspoon ground cardamom

$^1/_2$ scant cup rosewater *or* orange blossom water *or* boiled orange juice

2 tablespoons water

$1^3/_4$ cups confectioners' sugar

Preheat oven to 350°F. Line two or three baking sheets with parchment paper. Cream butter and sugar, then beat in egg and brandy. Combine nuts with sifted flour, baking powder, and cardamom. Add half nut mixture to butter; mix well. Add remaining nut mixture and gently bring together—don't overwork. Knead lightly on a bench for 10 seconds. Divide into six, roll each piece into a 4-inch-long log, and cut each log into ten. Take one piece at a time in your hands, roll into a cylinder with pointed ends, bend into a crescent, and place on a paper-lined baking sheet. (As you work keep remaining mixture covered with plastic to prevent it from drying out.) Bake until golden, 15 to 20 minutes. Remove to a wire rack.

Immediately brush the tops of the hot shortbread with combined rosewater and water. Leave for a minute, then dust liberally on both sides with sifted confectioners' sugar. Let cool completely. Store in an airtight container for up to 2 weeks.

Pumpkin seed oat shortbread

These are great served with Sticky Melon Jelly with Amaretti (see page 192), with poached stone fruit and mascarpone, or with a hard cheese such as pecorino sardo or a good cheddar.

Makes 32

- 1 cup (2 sticks) butter, at room temperature
- 3/4 cup superfine sugar
- 1 cup cornstarch
- 1 1/4 cups flour
- 1/2 cup quick oats
- 1/2 cup pumpkin seeds, lightly toasted

Preheat oven to 350°F. Line two baking sheets with parchment paper. Place butter and sugar in a food processor and process for 20 seconds. Scrape down the bowl, add remaining ingredients, and process for 10 seconds. Transfer to a bowl and gently bring together. Divide in half, then half again. Take each quarter and roll roughly into a 12-inch log, then take an eighth of each log and make it into any shape you want.

Place on baking sheets lined with parchment paper and cook until just beyond golden—about 12 minutes. Cool a little on the trays before transferring to a cake rack to cool completely.

Store in airtight container for up to 2 weeks.

Double chocolate mousse cake

This is my favorite chocolate cake. I have published the recipe before with the addition of star anise, but a collection of my favorite recipes wouldn't be complete without it. The double chocolate comes from covering the rich cake with ganache! Serve this with whipped cream, flavored with a little Cointreau, Tia Maria, chilled strong espresso, or rum.

Serves 8 to 10

- 10 1/2 oz dark chocolate
- 1/2 cup (1 stick) plus 3 tablespoons unsalted butter
- 6 eggs
- 1/2 cup superfine sugar

Preheat oven to 350°F. Line the base and sides of an 8-inch springform cake pan with parchment paper. Melt chocolate and butter in a metal bowl over a pan of simmering water. Separate eggs, and beat egg whites until stiff with 1/3 cup of the sugar. Beat yolks with remaining sugar, then mix this thoroughly into chocolate. Gently fold a third of the whites into chocolate mixture, then gently fold in the remainder. Pour into prepared tin and bake in the middle of the oven for 25 to 30 minutes. It's ready when a crust has formed, but the cake must be wobbly—if not, it'll be overcooked and set too hard.

Remove from the oven and cover tin tightly with foil—the steam keeps the heat in and softens the crust. Once cold, chill for at least 4 hours before removing from the pan and spreading the ganache on top. To cut, heat a sharp knife in a jug of hot water—it will slice more easily.

Ganache

- 8 oz chocolate
- 3/4 cup heavy cream, chilled

Melt chocolate in a metal bowl over simmering water, take off the heat, and stir in the cream. Spread over cake with a spatula to give an even coating.

Poppy seed, cinnamon, and orange palmiers

Poppy seed, cinnamon, and orange palmiers

I have made lavender palmiers many times, most notably at two wine events held in New Zealand's Hawke's Bay. I won't assume you'll be able to get edible lavender all year round, so this mixture comes a close second in the "yum yum stakes." These are best served with a creamy dessert, or alone with a strong coffee.

Makes 12

   1 puff pastry sheet, thawed

   3 tablespoons poppy seeds

   1 teaspoon ground cinnamon

   5 tablespoons confectioners' sugar

   finely grated zest of 1 orange

   1 tablespoon whole milk

   2 teaspoons superfine sugar

Unfold pastry sheet on a work surface. Place poppy seeds in a spice or coffee grinder and process 10 seconds. Transfer to a bowl. Add cinnamon, confectioners' sugar, and zest and mix well. Sprinkle evenly over pastry, lay a sheet of parchment paper over it, then gently roll a rolling pin backwards and forwards to press seed mixture into pastry. Take paper off, shaking any stray seeds back onto pastry. Fold narrow ends of pastry into the center, then fold one side over the other and gently pat down. Refrigerate and chill at least one hour.

   Preheat oven to 450°F. Line two baking sheets with parchment paper. Slice pastry into 12 pieces and lay these on two trays lined with parchment paper, leaving plenty of space for them to expand. Brush with milk and sprinkle with superfine sugar. Bake about 20 minutes or until golden and cooked all the way through. Cool on trays for a few minutes before removing to a cake rack. Store in an airtight container for up to 1 week.

Spiced apple, cheddar, and walnut rolls

Granny Smith and Golden Delicious apples work well for this, but make sure you use unsalted butter; otherwise the rolls will taste too salty.

Makes 12

   2 small apples, cored, peeled, and cut into
      1/2-inch cubes

   juice of 1 lemon

   1 scant cup confectioners' sugar

   1/2 cup grated cheddar

   1 teaspoon ground cinnamon

   1 teaspoon five spice powder

   1/2 teaspoon ground nutmeg

   3/4 cup walnuts, lightly toasted and roughly chopped

   4 sheets phyllo pastry

   1/2 scant cup (7 tablespoons) unsalted butter, melted

Preheat oven to 350°F. Line two baking sheets with parchment paper. Mix diced apple, lemon juice, and confectioners' sugar. Place on one of the trays and cook, turning occasionally, until apples are cooked through and lightly caramelized, about 30 minutes. Transfer to a bowl and mix in cheese, spices, and walnuts. Let cool.

   Cut phyllo sheets into three equal strips and lightly brush each strip with butter. Place one-twelfth apple mixture along the bottom of a strip in a thin sausage shape. Tightly roll pastry up into a cigarette shape, tucking the ends in to seal. Do the same with the rest of the mixture and the pastry. Place finished rolls on the second tray and brush with remaining butter. Bake until golden and crisp, about 20 minutes, then place on a cake rack and let cool. Store in an airtight jar for up to 2 days.

Lemon verbena and polenta cake with chocolate cardamom cream

Health shops often sell lemon verbena in "tea" form, if you're unable to find fresh leaves. If you are fortunate enough to have fresh leaves, dry them on the window ledge or in an airing cupboard. Either way, grind the verbena to a fine powder in a spice grinder or use a mortar and pestle. Failing that, use the finely grated zest of a lemon.

Makes one loaf, enough for 8 to 10

- $1/3$ heaping cup superfine sugar
- 2 eggs
- 2 teaspoons powdered lemon verbena
- $1/2$ cup light olive oil
- $1/2$ cup sweet white wine
- 1 scant cup flour
- $11/2$ teaspoons baking powder
- $1/2$ cup polenta

Preheat oven to 400°F. Line a loaf pan with parchment paper. Beat superfine sugar, eggs, and lemon verbena together until pale-colored and fluffy. Lightly whisk in oil and wine. Sieve flour, baking powder, and polenta together and gently stir in. Pour batter into prepared loaf pan and bake in the center of the oven for 15 minutes, then cover the pan loosely with foil and turn the oven down to 350°F. Bake another 25 minutes. Test by inserting a skewer into the deepest part. It should come out a little moist but clean. Remove the foil and cool on a cake rack.

To serve, slice cake and dollop on chocolate cardamom cream. This is also excellent served with poached pears or stone fruit.

Chocolate cardamom cream

- $21/2$ oz dark chocolate (60 to 70 percent cacao butter)
- $1/4$ teaspoon powdered cardamom
- 1 scant cup cream, chilled
- 1 tablespoon superfine sugar

Melt chocolate with cardamom in a heatproof bowl (or microwave), take off the heat, and add a quarter of the cream and all of the sugar. Stir well. Once chocolate has cooled, but before it sets, add remaining cream and whisk all together until it forms soft peaks.

Boiled orange, almond, and rosewater cake

The addition of rosewater gives this "old favorite" a Middle Eastern flavor. This very moist dessert cake is good served with cream and a strong espresso.

Serves 8 to 10

> **3 small to medium oranges**
>
> **1^1/$_3$ cups superfine sugar**
>
> **2^1/$_2$ cups almonds, ground**
>
> **6 eggs**
>
> **2 teaspoons baking powder**
>
> **^{1}/$_2$ scant cup rosewater**
>
> **^{2}/$_3$ cup orange juice**
>
> **zest of 1 orange, julienned**
>
> **^{2}/$_3$ cup white sugar**

Preheat oven to 350°F. Line a 9- or 10-inch springform cake pan with parchment paper. Wipe oranges well and place in a deep saucepan with enough cold water to cover. Bring to a boil and cook with the lid on for 20 minutes. Remove from the pan and cool for 20 minutes. Cut in half and remove any seeds, then place in a food processor, skin and all. Add superfine sugar and process for 30 seconds. Add almonds, eggs, baking powder, and half the rosewater and purée for 10 seconds. Scrape down the sides of the bowl and purée for another 10 seconds. Pour the mixture into the pan and bake 60 minutes. Check after 50 minutes by inserting a skewer into the center of the cake. It should come out slightly moist, but if you think it needs more cooking, cover the pan with foil and cook until done.

Cool for 30 minutes in the pan before removing and placing on a plate. Meanwhile, bring orange juice, zest, and sugar to a boil, simmer until syrupy, then remove from the heat and add remaining rosewater. Prick the top of the cake 20 times with a skewer and spoon the syrup over.

Rhubarb and ginger tart

This can be served straight from the oven but is best left to rest for an hour or more and served at room temperature with whipped cream or vanilla ice cream.

Makes one 12-inch tart

4 eggs

1 scant cup golden syrup

1 scant cup runny honey

1²/₃ cups cream

¹/₂ lb rhubarb, split down the middle, then finely sliced

1³/₄ heaped cups fresh breadcrumbs

1 heaped tablespoon candied ginger, finely chopped

12-inch Sweet Nutty Pastry shell, partially cooked

Preheat oven to 350°F. Beat eggs with golden syrup and honey for a minute, then add cream and beat for another 10 seconds. Mix in rhubarb, breadcrumbs, and ginger and mix well. Pour into pastry shell, place on a baking sheet, and bake about 50 minutes. The tart is cooked when the filling has turned golden and slightly puffy.

Sweet nutty pastry

The following is based on an Alastair Little recipe, which, in turn, was inspired by a recipe of Roger Verge's in Cuisine of the Sun. *It will make two shells, which freeze well and can be cooked straight from the freezer without baking it first. What I like about it is that you don't actually roll out the pastry, you just slice it and press it into the pan.*

¹/₂ cup superfine sugar

¹/₂ cup almonds, ground

pinch salt

2¹/₄ cups plain flour

1 cup (2 sticks) plus 1 tablespoon unsalted butter, diced into cubes

1 whole egg, plus 1 extra yolk

¹/₂ teaspoon grated lemon zest

2 teaspoons vodka *or* gin *or* pure vanilla extract

Put sugar, almonds, salt, and flour into a food processor and process for a few seconds. Add butter and process again until just blended in. The mixture will resemble fine breadcrumbs. Add egg and extra yolk, lemon zest, and alcohol and process again until the dough just combines. Transfer to a sheet of plastic wrap, gently knead for a few seconds only, then roll up to form a cylinder with a diameter of 2¹/₂ to 3 inches. Chill for at least 3 hours before using.

To use, simply take from the fridge, let soften for 10 minutes, then slice into ¹/₈-inch-thick disks and place these in the tart pan, slightly overlapping. Press them together to fill in any spaces and try to make it reasonably even. Place back in the fridge for 45 minutes (or 20 minutes in a freezer) before baking at 350°F. You won't need to bake it using beans and foil unless you're making a very deep tart that is more than 2¹/₂ inches deep.

Pineapple, cashew, and cardamom tart

This slightly tropical tart makes the depths of London's winter seem more bearable. Serve warm with whipped cream, crème fraîche, or vanilla ice cream.

Makes one 12-inch tart

- 1 small pineapple
- 2 cups pineapple juice
- 1 cup cashew nuts, lightly toasted
- 7 tablespoons unsalted butter
- 1 cup confectioners' sugar
- $1^1/_2$ teaspoons ground cardamom
- 2 eggs
- 2 tablespoons flour
- 3 tablespoons rum
- 1 partially cooked (12-inch) Sweet Nutty Pastry shell (see recipe on page 178)

Peel and quarter pineapple. Remove core and slice into pieces $1/_2$ inch thick. Place in a saucepan (not aluminium), add pineapple juice, and bring to a boil. Turn heat to a rapid simmer and cook until juice has almost evaporated. Let cool.

Preheat oven to 350°F. Place cashew nuts in a food processor and process to a fine crumb. Add butter, confectioners' sugar, and cardamom and process 10 seconds. Add eggs, flour, and rum and process to a thick paste. Spread evenly in partially cooked pastry shell. Lay pineapple on top, pressing in gently. Bake until nut mixture is cooked through, about 40 minutes—test with a skewer.

Passion fruit coconut cream tart

The sharpness of passion fruit works really well when it's mixed with sugar or cream, and here it is combined with both in a sweet, creamy tart.

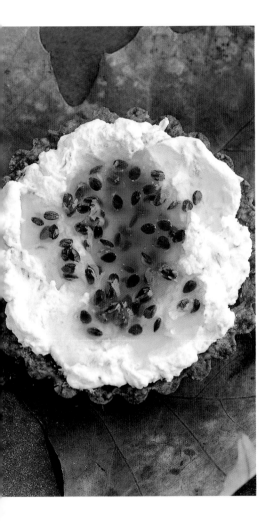

Makes one 12-inch or eight 3-inch tarts

1 portion Sweet Nutty Pastry (see recipe on page 178)

1 cup passion fruit pulp (about 12 to 15 fruit)

3/4 cup superfine sugar

1 1/4 cups heavy cream

1 scant cup mascarpone *or* cream cheese

1/4 cup demerara *or* raw sugar

3/4 cup shredded coconut, oven toasted until golden

1 capful pure vanilla extract

Once pastry has firmed in the fridge for at least 3 hours, cut it into slices about 1/8 to 1/4 inch thick and lay, slightly overlapping, in a 12-inch loose-bottomed tart pan or individual pans. Press down to fill in any gaps and to make the shell as even as possible. Prick the center several times with a fork. Place back in the fridge or freezer to chill for 30 minutes and turn the oven to 350°F. Bake on the middle shelf of the oven until fully cooked and golden. Remove and let cool.

Meanwhile, place passion fruit pulp and sugar in a small pan and bring to a boil. Simmer 4 to 5 minutes until thickish and syrupy. Let cool completely.

Just before serving, place cream, mascarpone, and sugar in a bowl and whip until soft peaks form. Add coconut and vanilla and mix in until firm. Spoon cream into the cold tart shell and even it out, then add the cold passion fruit mixture on top.

Banoffee pie

This incredibly rich pie takes its name from the bananas and toffee used to make it. I first tasted it in a café on London's Portobello Road back in 1990, where I was surprised to see the toffee my Gran had used in her Caramel Shortbread Slice used in something quite different. You can make the condensed milk toffee up to a month in advance; just keep it unopened in a cool place.

Serves 10 to 12

2 (14-oz) cans sweetened condensed milk

1 lb digestive biscuits *or* graham crackers

1 cup (2 sticks) unsalted butter, melted

3 to 4 bananas, ripe but not beginning to brown

whipped cream to serve

Remove labels from the condensed milk cans. Use a can opener to make small punctures on opposite sides of the top of the can. Place the cans in a large deep saucepan puncture side up, fill with hot water two-thirds of the way up the cans, and bring to a boil. Place lid on pan, lower the heat until the water simmers, and cook two hours. Check from time to time that the water hasn't evaporated below the level of the cans and top up with hot water if necessary. A bit of milk may seep out the small holes in the can. (Do not boil the can unopened as a shortcut. The milk expands when heated and may erupt with explosive results.) Take off the heat and let cool—about 4 hours at room temperature. Please be careful when handling these hot cans, as they retain their heat for a long, long time.

Make the pie crust by grinding the cookies in a food processor to a fine crumb. Pour in melted butter while the motor is still running, then transfer the contents into a bowl and mix well. Spread over base and sides of a 2-inch deep, 9½-inch springform cake pan. Place in the fridge to firm up.

Open both cans of the cooled, caramelized milk and pour into a bowl, mix well to soften it up, then spread one-fifth of the mixture over the bottom of the pie crust. Peel and slice the bananas ½ inch thick.

Spread slices evenly in the pan and press into the caramel. Spoon remaining caramel on top of bananas and smooth it over with the back of a spoon. Cover the pie with plastic wrap and chill for at least 3 hours before eating. Serve with whipped cream.

cool desserts

Cool desserts are the things I crave in summer. Something made with a lot of summer fruit—berries and stone fruits—or maybe something more tropical such as mango or passion fruit. Ice creams come to the fore in summer; here I've given recipes not just for ice cream machine-made delicacies but also frozen desserts you can make using just the freezer. In the height of summer, the perfect dessert may just be a plate of chilled melon and raspberries, but with a little more effort you can throw together something more stunning and exciting.

Grilled mango and coconut sandwich with banana cream

There are many steps in making this dish, but it will make a great ending to your dinner party if you want to impress. All the steps are quite simple in themselves—it's in the assembly that it begins to look complicated. You will end up with more coconut wafers than you need, but the mixture will keep in the fridge for a week, and cooked wafers will keep in an airtight jar for two weeks.

Serves 4

Coconut wafers

3 cups shredded coconut

1$^1/_2$ scant cups superfine sugar

$^1/_3$ cup flour

1 cup egg whites, (about 8 large eggs)

7 tablespoons melted butter

Preheat oven to 350°F. Combine coconut, superfine sugar, and flour and stir in egg whites. Mix in butter and stand for 30 minutes. Lightly grease baking sheets or line with parchment paper. Dollop a tablespoonful of coconut mixture on the tray and spread out to a mango shape. Add a little more mixture if needed, but keep the wafers very thin. You will need to make 12 wafers for this dessert. Leave 1$^1/_4$ inches between each one. Bake for 8 to 10 minutes or until golden brown, then cool for 30 seconds before removing to a cake rack.

Banana cream

$^3/_4$ cup superfine sugar

1$^1/_2$ tablespoons water

1 large ripe banana, peeled and cut into $^1/_2$-inch chunks

2 tablespoons lemon juice

1$^2/_3$ cups cream

Bring sugar and water to a boil, then cook without stirring until it turns golden. Once it begins to give off a caramel aroma, carefully but quickly add banana pieces and lemon juice. Stir carefully, as it will be viciously hot and may splatter. Cook 1$^1/_2$ minutes on high heat, mashing the bananas as you go. Remove from heat and let cool, then chill. Beat cream until soft peaks form, then add banana mixture and whip until fairly stiff. This keeps in the fridge for up to 4 hours.

Grilled mango

2 medium to large ripe mangoes

$^1/_2$ cup demerara *or* raw sugar

Peel mangoes with either a small sharp knife or potato peeler, then halve them by slicing the lobes off each side of the pit. Lay mangoes on a cutting board, cut side down, and cut in half horizontally. Place on an oiled, foil-lined baking sheet and sprinkle with sugar. Place under a broiler, about 1$^1/_4$ to 2 inches from the heat, and cook until sugar caramelizes and mango begins to color. Allow to cool.

To assemble

Place a small teaspoon of the cream on four plates and set a wafer on top of each. Place an eighth of the cream on each wafer and smooth it out, then set the flatter pieces of mango on top. Set a wafer on these and again spread some banana cream on top, set the rounded pieces of mango on next, then balance the last wafers on top. Serve with a lime wedge to complement the taste of the mango and to cut through the richness of this dessert.

Frozen Amaretto, fruit, and nut parfait

While technically not a real parfait, this is close enough—and it looks and tastes divine. Fresh or frozen (unthawed) raspberries can be used, and it can be made two days in advance.

1/2 cup sweet raisins

3 tablespoons Amaretto liqueur

3 1/3 cups cream

1 scant cup light runny honey, at room temperature

2 cups raspberries

3/4 cup flaked almonds, lightly toasted

1 cup pistachios, hulled and lightly toasted

8 amaretti biscuits *or* bitter almond cookies, roughly crushed

Soak raisins in Amaretto liqueur for 2 hours, stirring occasionally. Line a large loaf pan with a double thickness of plastic wrap, making sure there is at least a 4-inch overhang on all sides. Place tin in the freezer.

Whip cream and honey together to form peaks, not too soft, not too firm. Fold in soaked raisins, liqueur, raspberries, and nuts. Pour into the loaf pan, then sprinkle with biscuits. Fold the plastic wrap over and gently press down to seal. Freeze for at least 8 hours.

To serve, cut the parfait into slices and serve with some extra berries.

Kerry Fox's favorite cherry ripple ice cream

Our good friend Kerry Fox loves the cherry ripple ice cream I used to make, so this recipe is for her. It takes quite a while to make this, but you can speed it up if you use an ice cream machine.

Serves 8 to 10

1 1/4 cups cream

2 cups milk

1/2 cup golden syrup

1 cup superfine sugar

8 egg yolks

2 1/2 to 3 cups ripe cherries, pitted and washed, *or* canned cherries, drained

Bring cream, milk, and golden syrup to a boil. (The mixture may look curdled, but this will not affect the final result.) Beat half the superfine sugar and egg yolks together for 30 seconds. Whisk cream mixture into the yolks, then return to the pan and cook over a moderate heat, stirring continually, until it coats the back of a spoon. Don't overcook or it will curdle. Strain into a clean bowl and let cool completely, then pour into a shallow metal tray and place in the freezer. It will take 4 to 8 hours to fully freeze depending on the power of your freezer. You'll need to stir it every few hours to break up the ice lumps as they form, so it's a long process. You could also freeze it in an ice cream maker.

Meanwhile, place cherries and remaining superfine sugar in a deep saucepan and cook over a moderate heat until a thick syrup forms. Cool, then place in the refrigerator.

Once ice cream has frozen solid, remove from the freezer and scoop half into a food processor. Pulse to break up ice crystals, then transfer to a chilled bowl and do the same with the other half. Fold in the cold cherries and their syrup, being careful not to overmix—you do want a ripple effect, after all. Place in a 2-quart container, return to the freezer, and freeze until set.

Chocolate, rum, and pecan ice cream

If chocolate is added to an ice cream mixture, it will be quite hard when it freezes, so here I have added rum (as alcohol doesn't freeze) to compensate. This "adults only" dessert can be made in an ice cream machine or a food processor.

Serves 6 to 8

- 1^2/$_3$ cups cream
- 1^2/$_3$ cups milk
- 3 tablespoons light honey
- 8 egg yolks
- ^{1}/$_2$ scant cup demerara *or* raw sugar
- 2 tablespoons cocoa, sifted
- 5 oz dark chocolate, roughly chopped or grated
- ^{1}/$_2$ scant cup dark rum
- 1^3/$_4$ cups pecan nuts, lightly toasted and roughly chopped

Bring cream, milk, and honey to a boil. Meanwhile, whisk yolks, sugar, and cocoa together until mixture forms ribbons. Slowly pour half the hot cream mixture onto yolks, whisking all the time, then pour back into the saucepan and cook gently over a moderate heat until thick enough to coat the back of a spoon. Do not boil or it will curdle. Strain into a clean bowl and add chocolate. Stir until it has melted, then cool. Mix in rum and churn in an ice cream machine to manufacturer's instructions. Remove mixture from machine and stir in nuts before transferring to a container and freezing.

If you don't have a machine, make as above to the point where you add the rum, then pour into a shallow tray and freeze, stirring the ice crystals that form from the outside into the middle. When completely frozen, break it up, place in a food processor, and pulse into a thick mush. Stir in nuts, transfer to a container, and refreeze.

Chocolate-stuffed prunes with Calvados and ice cream

When I first arrived in London in 1989, every restaurant seemed to be serving prune and Armagnac ice cream. This is a slight play on that, with the addition of another perfect combination—jaffa (orange and chocolate). You can also serve these prunes individually with coffee after a meal.

Serves 4

- 3^1/$_2$ oz dark chocolate, finely grated or chopped
- finely grated zest of 1 orange
- 12 pitted prunes
- 3 tablespoons Calvados (apple brandy)
- 4 scoops vanilla ice cream

Combine chocolate and orange zest. Take each prune and poke your finger into the cavity to widen it. Stuff with jaffa mixture and then fold prune back over itself to seal. Place prunes in a saucepan just large enough to hold them, holes facing upwards. Pour in enough warm water to come halfway up prunes. Cover and bring to a simmer. After 2 minutes check they haven't boiled dry, then continue to cook until there is barely any water left. Add Calvados, put the lid back on, and let cool. To serve, place a scoop of ice cream in a dish, add three prunes, and pour some syrup on top.

Spiced poached quince

Quince are very dense and delicious if cooked slowly with lots of sugar. If you can't get any, cook pears in a similar way (but halve cooking time). These are really good with vanilla ice cream and a crunchy cookie such as biscotti. And be sure to make extra to use on a Chicken, Spiced Quince, and Hummus Burger (page 130).

1/2 fresh red chile

2/3 cup light honey

1 1/3 cups superfine sugar

1 bay leaf

3 cups plus 1 tablespoon red wine (any variety)

3/4 cup red wine vinegar

2 star anise

6 quince

Place everything except the quince in a saucepan just large enough to hold all the fruit. Peel quince, adding peel from one fruit to the pan (it's a good idea to wear gloves as they can make your hands sticky). Halve fruit and scoop out cores with a teaspoon or melon-baller. Add quince to the pan, along with scooped-out cores. Bring to a boil, then turn to a simmer; add boiling water if necessary to ensure the fruit is fully submerged. Cut a circle of parchment paper just larger than the circumference of the pan and place on top of fruit, then place the lid on. Simmer 40 to 60 minutes (30 minutes for pears). Test by poking the quince with a fine sharp knife or skewer—it should go through quite easily. Cool completely, then carefully transfer quince into a clean resealable container and strain the liquid over them. Store in the fridge. (This will keep for 4 weeks if the fruit is fully submerged.)

Crème brûlée with raspberries

I really enjoy the simplicity of a crème brûlée, but the addition in this version of some tart raspberries gives a sexy twist.

Makes 6

3 3/4 cups heavy cream

1 scant cup superfine sugar

1/2 vanilla bean, split lengthways, seeds scraped out

9 egg yolks

24 raspberries

2/3 cup demerara *or* raw sugar

Preheat oven to 325°F. Make a bain-marie by placing a roasting dish on a shelf in the middle of the oven and pouring in boiling water to a depth of 1 1/4 inches. You'll need six 1-cup ceramic ramekins for this recipe.

Place cream, half the sugar, and vanilla bean in a saucepan and bring gently to a boil. Remove from heat, cover, and allow to sit for 10 minutes.

Lightly whisk yolks with remaining sugar. Gradually add hot cream, whisking well, then pour through a sieve into a clean container.

Put four raspberries in the base of each ramekin, then pour in the cream mixture. Place ramekins in the bain-marie and bake for 30 to 45 minutes or until a skewer comes out clean. If you notice that the crèmes are bubbling in their dishes, the oven is too hot, so open the door and pour half a cup of very cold water into the bain-marie to cool it down a little.

Once cooked, turn the oven off and very carefully take the bain-marie from the oven (the roasting dish is full of very hot water, so be careful). Remove ramekins from the bain-marie and cool on a wire rack for 30 minutes. Refrigerate, covered, for 4 or more hours until they have set firm.

Just before serving, sprinkle sugar in a thin layer on top of each brûlée. Place under a very hot broiler, or use a cook's blowtorch, until a thin layer of caramel forms. Keep an eye on them, as they will go from sugar to burned toffee quite quickly. Stand 1 minute before serving, as the toffee will burn your lips.

Crème brûlée with raspberries

Orange honey crème brûlée

Crème brûlée works so well because it has a delicious brittle layer of toffee on top of a soft creamy base. The orange and honey in this recipe add a little twist to a wonderful classic.

Makes 6

3/4 cup runny light honey

2 3/4 cups heavy cream

1 cup milk

finely grated zest of 2 oranges

1/2 vanilla bean, split lengthways, seeds scraped out

9 egg yolks

3 to 4 tablespoons demerara *or* raw sugar

Preheat oven to 300°F. Make a bain-marie by placing a roasting dish on a shelf in the middle of the oven and pouring in boiling water to a depth of 1 1/4 inches.

Place honey, cream, milk, orange zest, and vanilla bean and seeds in a saucepan and bring gently to a boil. Remove from heat, cover, and allow to infuse for 10 minutes.

Bring cream back to a simmer. Lightly whisk egg yolks. Slowly pour hot cream onto yolks, whisking as you go, then pour mixture through a sieve.

Divide mixture between six 1-cup ramekins and carefully place in the roasting tray. If necessary, add extra boiling water to the roasting pan so that it comes three-quarters of the way up the sides of the ramekins. Bake 35 minutes. The crèmes should still be slightly wobbly. If you notice that the crèmes are bubbling in their dishes, the oven is too hot, so open the door and pour half a cup of very cold water into the bain-marie to cool it down a little.

Once cooked, turn the oven off and very carefully take the bain-marie from the oven (the roasting dish is full of very hot water, so be careful). Remove ramekins from the bain-marie and cool on a wire rack for 30 minutes. Refrigerate for 4 or more hours, covered, until they have set firm.

Just before serving, sprinkle sugar in a thin layer on top of each brûlée. Place under a very hot broiler or use a cook's blowtorch, until a thin layer of caramel forms. Keep an eye on them, as they will go from sugar to burned toffee quite quickly. Stand 1 minute before serving, as the toffee will burn your lips.

Coconut, cardamom, and coffee crème brûlée

This surprising third version uses "exotic" ingredients to give this classic French dessert a feel of the Far East.

Makes 4

2^1/$_2$ **cups heavy cream**

^{1}/$_2$ **teaspoon ground cardamom**

finely ground coffee

1^1/$_4$ **cups shredded coconut ground in a spice grinder to a fine powder**

^{3}/$_4$ **cup unrefined superfine sugar**

6 egg yolks

demerara *or* **raw sugar for glazing**

Preheat oven to 325°F. Make a bain-marie by placing a roasting dish on a shelf in the middle of the oven and pouring in boiling water to a depth of 1^1/$_4$ inches. You'll need four 1-cup ceramic ramekins for this recipe.

Place cream, cardamom, coffee, coconut, and half the sugar in a saucepan and bring gently to a boil. Remove from heat, cover, and allow to infuse for 10 minutes. Lightly whisk yolks with the remaining sugar for 20 seconds, then slowly pour in the hot cream, mixing well. Strain into a clean container.

Divide mixture between the ramekins and carefully place in a roasting pan with enough hot water to come two-thirds up the sides. Bake 1 hour. (If you notice that the crèmes are bubbling in their dishes, the oven is too hot, so open the door and pour half a cup of very cold water into the bain-marie to cool it down a little.)

Once cooked, turn the oven off and very carefully take the bain-marie from the oven (the roasting dish is full of very hot water, so be careful). Remove ramekins from the bain-marie and cool on a wire rack for 30 minutes. Refrigerate, covered, for 4 or more hours until they have set firm.

Just before serving, sprinkle sugar in a thin layer on top of each brûlée. Place under a very hot broiler or use a cook's blowtorch, until a thin layer of caramel forms. Keep an eye on them, as they will go from sugar to burned toffee quite quickly. Stand 1 minute before serving, as the toffee will burn your lips.

Sticky melon jelly with amaretti

Here, dessert wines are often called "stickies," due to their residual sugars, which make them so luscious. Serve this lovely dessert with Pumpkin Seed Oat Shortbread (see page 173), which makes a great crunchy accompaniment.

Makes 8

- **1 small orange-fleshed melon**
- **1 small white *or* pink-fleshed melon**
- **3¹/₃ cups fresh apple *or* melon juice, chilled**
- **8 sheets leaf gelatin *or* 2 oz powdered gelatine**
- **1 cup dessert wine**
- **12 amaretti biscuits *or* bitter almond cookies, crushed**

To make this you will need eight 1-cup jelly molds or metal ramekins, or one large jelly ring mold. Use a melon-baller (a teaspoon will work at a pinch) to scoop out about 16 balls from each melon. Keep them chilled in the fridge.

Pour juice into a shallow dish and lay gelatin leaves in, one at a time. Soak for 5 minutes until soft. Meanwhile, place wine in a saucepan and bring to a boil, then simmer 2 minutes. Remove gelatin leaves from juice, drain them a little by squeezing them gently in your hand, then add them to the hot wine and mix to dissolve. Let cool 5 minutes, then add the juice to the wine, mix well, and pour into a container.

If using powdered gelatin, sprinkle it over the juice in a bowl and let soak for 5 minutes. Simmer the wine as above, then simply pour the dissolved gelatin and juice into the hot wine and stir, making sure there are no lumps. Mix well and pour into a container.

Place two melon balls of each color into jelly molds and pour on just enough jelly to cover and allow the balls to float. Place on a tray in the fridge to cool completely until set. Place the rest of the jelly in the fridge as well.

Once the first layer has barely set, sprinkle the amaretti evenly over jellies and gently pour or spoon remaining cooled jelly on top. Let set completely, then cover the tray with plastic wrap. Eat within 2 days.

Marinated strawberry and papaya salad

This incredibly simple, "no-cook" dessert is great served on its own or with lightly whipped cream and biscotti.

Serves 6 to 8

- **2 lb strawberries**
- **¹/₂ cup dessert wine**
- **1 ripe medium-sized papaya**
- **20 small mint leaves**
- **2 tablespoons lime juice**

Remove green tops from strawberries and cut in half lengthwise. Place in a bowl, pour wine on top, and gently mix. Cover and refrigerate 1 to 2 hours, gently tossing twice more during this time.

Meanwhile, peel and halve papaya. Remove seeds and cut flesh roughly into ³/₄-inch chunks. Mix with mint leaves and lime juice and marinate, covered, in the fridge.

To serve, gently toss the papaya and divide between four dishes, juice and all. Toss strawberries one last time and place these on top, then splash the juices over the fruit.

Marinated orange slices with vanilla yogurt

This really couldn't be simpler. Apart from dissolving the sugar, it requires no cooking and is best made eight to twenty-four hours before you want to eat it.

Serves 4

  1 cup superfine sugar

  1 1/2 cups water

  1 teaspoon whole rosemary leaves

  zest of 1 orange, julienned

  3 oranges

  1/3 cup rosewater

  1/2 vanilla bean *or* 1/2 teaspoon real vanilla extract

  1/2 scant cup thick yogurt

  1/2 scant cup cream

To make marinade, place sugar and a third of the water in a saucepan with rosemary and orange zest. Bring to a boil and simmer 2 minutes. Pour into a large bowl. Add remaining water, then let cool.

Peel oranges with a sharp knife, removing all pith. Cut into slices about 1/3 inch thick (any thinner and they fall apart; any thicker and they don't take on the flavor so well). Stir marinade well, add rosewater, and gently toss oranges in it. Cover with plastic wrap and chill. After 2 hours, toss gently to make sure oranges absorb the flavors evenly.

To make vanilla yogurt, scrape seeds from vanilla bean and whisk into yogurt and cream until soft peaks form. Spoon over oranges and their juice when serving.

Berry bavarois

This dessert is an easy-to-make "mousse." You can make it in a couple of minutes using a food processor, but it will require a few hours in the fridge to cool and become firm. Use berries that are full of flavor to make the purée. One pound of assorted berries will yield about 1¹/2 cups of purée. I used equal quantities of strawberries and raspberries.

Makes 4

> 3 (¹/4-oz) packets powdered gelatin *or* 2³/4 gelatin
>   leaves
> 3 tablespoons water
> 1¹/2 cups fresh berry purée
> 1¹/3 cups confectioners' sugar
> 1 cup Greek-style yogurt
> 1¹/2 cups cream, lightly whipped

If using powdered gelatin, sprinkle it over the water in a bowl, stir, and let soak for 10 minutes. Dissolve it by either microwaving on high for 30 to 40 seconds or placing the bowl over a pan of simmering water and stirring to dissolve. If using leaf gelatin, soak the leaves in a flat tray of cold water ¹/2 inch deep. Soak for 2 to 3 minutes, then squeeze the water out and stir into 3 tablespoons of very hot water. Place gelatin, berry purée, confectioners' sugar, and yogurt in a food processor or blender and purée for 1 minute. Transfer to a large bowl, gently fold in cream, then pour into four 1¹/2-cup jelly molds. Chill at least 2 hours. Serve with fresh berries and extra whipped cream on the side.

Panettone and mascarpone cake with berries and cherries

Panettone is a large, round Italian cake. The dough is enriched with egg yolks; then raisins and candied peel are added. A light sponge cake can be substituted here.

Serves 8

> 1 (1-lb) panettone
> 1 lb mascarpone
> 2 cups heavy *or* whipping cream
> 1³/4 cups confectioners' sugar, plus extra for garnish
> 1 lb raspberries
> ²/3 lb strawberries, hulled and halved
> ²/3 lb pitted cherries

Slice panettone horizontally into four rings, then place the bottom piece on a serving plate. Whisk mascarpone, cream, and confectioners' sugar until soft peaks begin to form. Add half the raspberries and beat until quite firm. Mix the remaining berries and cherries together. Spread a third of the cream on the base and scatter a third of the berries and cherries on top. Lay another slice of panettone on top and repeat until you have reassembled the cake. Cover and chill for 2 hours. To serve, dust panettone with extra icing sugar and then cut it into wedges.

Panettone and mascarpone cake with berries and cherries

Passion fruit panna cotta

Panna cotta is Italian for "cooked cream." It is much like a bavarois, without eggs, and very little skill is required. It should always be wobbly in texture. Traditionally, it is made from vanilla-flavored cream and milk, but this twist is really lovely.

Serves 8

> 1 cup superfine sugar
>
> $3/4$ cup fresh passion fruit pulp (6 to 8 large passion fruit)
>
> 1 vanilla bean, split in half, then cut into 4
>
> $4^2/3$ cups milk
>
> 3 cups heavy cream
>
> 8 leaves gelatin *or* 9 ($1/4$-oz) packets powdered gelatin
>
> $3/4$ cup cold water

Place sugar, passion fruit pulp, and vanilla bean in a pan and bring to a boil; simmer for 1 minute. Add milk and cream, bring back almost to a boil, whisking gently, then remove from heat. Strain the seeds out if you prefer (but they look good and provide a little texture).

If using gelatin leaves, soak them in cold water for 4 minutes before squeezing out excess water and adding the leaves (with none of the water) to the hot mixture. If using powdered gelatin, then sprinkle it over $1/2$ cup warm water in a small bowl and let soak for 5 minutes, stir, and then mix into the hot mixture, making sure there are no lumps. Pour the mixture into eight 1-cup metal ramekins or one 8-cup mold. Cool, then cover and refrigerate to set (about 4 hours for ramekins or 8 hours for a large mold).

To unmold, dip the molds briefly into a bowl of very hot water, then invert onto a plate.

(Photograph of recipe on page 4.)

Kiwi and passion fruit fool

I guess a fool is so called because even a fool could make one. The only trick is that the fruit must be sharp and slightly acidic so that the cream acts as a foil, providing a creamy mask to bring it all together. However, I've also made a delicious fool using very sweet apricots, where I added tang to the cream by mixing in very sharp ewes' milk yogurt. Again, it was the contrast of sharp and creamy that pulled it off.

Makes 4

> 4 kiwi
>
> 1 tablespoon lemon *or* lime juice
>
> $1^1/2$ cups heavy *or* whipping cream
>
> $1/2$ cup thick yogurt
>
> 3 tablespoons confectioners' sugar
>
> 4 passion fruit

Peel kiwi and cut lengthways into quarters, then slice into $1/4$-inch-thick pieces. Mix with citrus juice and refrigerate 5 minutes.

Place cream, yogurt, and confectioners' sugar in a bowl and whip to form just-past-soft peaks. Divide half the cream between four glasses, then spoon in kiwi. Place remaining cream in glasses, then spoon passion fruit pulp on top. Chill 5 minutes before serving. Serve with a wafer or biscotti to add some crunchy texture.

Coconut meringues with raspberry and pineapple salad

These meringues can be made two days in advance. You could marinate the pineapple the day before, then just quickly finish the dessert on the day.

For 6 to 8

- $3/4$ cup egg whites (about 6 large eggs)
- $2^2/3$ cups confectioners' sugar
- 1 teaspoon lemon juice
- 1 teaspoon vanilla extract
- pinch salt
- $1^1/2$ cups shredded coconut
- $1/2$ small, very ripe pineapple
- $1/2$ cup sweet dessert wine
- $2/3$ lb raspberries
- $1^1/2$ cups heavy *or* whipping cream
- $1/2$ cup yogurt

Preheat oven to 210°F. Place egg whites in a bowl with confectioners' sugar, lemon juice, vanilla, and salt. Beat on high with a balloon whisk for 12 minutes until glossy and very stiff. Fold in coconut. Line one or two baking sheets with parchment paper and dollop on 8 lumps of meringue mixture (allow for breakages), leaving space in between. Use the back of a spoon to make a hollow in each one. Bake until dry—about 2 hours.

Peel, core, and quarter pineapple, then cut into thin pieces. Mix with wine in a bowl and marinate at least 3 hours. Add berries.

Beat cream with yogurt until soft peaks form. Add a few tablespoons of pineapple marinade and beat to firmer peaks. To serve, dollop some cream into each meringue, then spoon fruit on top and pour the wine marinade over each.

Gooseberry and coffee compote with pistachio cream

You have to have the cream with this or else you won't like it—it's the cream reacting with the coffee that makes it work. This recipe came about when I accidentally dropped some coffee grounds into some gooseberries. Now I pretend that it was an inspiration!

Serves 4

- $1/2$ cup superfine sugar
- 1 heaped teaspoon finely ground coffee *or* instant coffee if you'd prefer not to eat the grains
- 1 scant cup water
- 1 lb gooseberries *or* cranberries, washed
- $1/2$ cup shelled pistachio nuts
- $1/2$ scant cup confectioners' sugar
- $1^1/4$ cups heavy cream

Place sugar, coffee, and water in a wide, shallow pan and bring to a boil, stirring to dissolve sugar. Add gooseberries, turn the heat to medium, then cook until the first gooseberries burst, gently shaking the pan from time to time. Let cool.

Place nuts and confectioners' sugar in a food processor and process to a fine powder. Add three-quarters of the nut mixture to cream and whip until soft peaks form. Chill.

To serve, spoon gooseberries and syrup into a glass dish, dollop on some cream, then sprinkle with nut mixture.

Fruit cake crème with raspberries and almonds

I first made this at a demonstration I did in London on "a typical New Zealand Christmas meal," when I tried to think of a way to make such a rich cake appealing in a hot New Zealand summer. I really fell for it and have made it many times since. It's a good way to serve fruit cake in disguise and is best served really chilled.

Serves 6

2/3 lb fruit cake

33/4 cups cream

2/3 cup superfine sugar

9 egg yolks

1/2 teaspoon pure vanilla extract

11/2 cups raspberries

flaked almonds, toasted

cream to serve

Preheat oven to 350°F. Divide cake between six oven-proof glasses (about 1 cup in volume), pressing it firmly into the bottom. Bring cream and half the sugar to a boil. Whisk yolks with remaining sugar and vanilla and gradually pour on the hot cream, whisking as you go. Pour cream through a sieve into a clean container, then pour onto the cake in the glasses.

Place a deep roasting dish in the center of the oven, place the glasses in the dish, and fill with enough hot water to come three-quarters of the way up the sides of the glasses. Place in the center of the oven and bake for 35 to 45 minutes until the custard has set on top and looks a little firm but still has a slight wobble. Take the roasting dish out of the oven and let cool completely before removing the custards. Cover with plastic wrap and refrigerate for at least 6 hours.

To serve, pile raspberries and almonds on the custards and serve with cream.

Barbecued figs on toasted fruit cake with ice cream

If, like me, you have a few pounds of assorted Christmas cakes hanging around in December and January, this is a good way to use them up. Of course, Christmas occurs in summer in the Southern Hemisphere and in winter in the north. So, Antipodeans can make this with figs, but in the north we'll have to use pears or imported pineapple.

Serves 4

4 large or 6 small figs *or* 1/2 ripe pineapple

2 teaspoons cooking oil

4 slices fruit cake, about 2/3 inch thick

vanilla ice cream

confectioners' sugar for dusting

Cut figs in half lengthwise and brush with a little oil. Grill on the cut side over a hot part of the barbecue or in a heavy skillet until dark golden in color (they will stick a little to the grill). Turn over and cook on the other side for about 1 minute.

While they're cooking, toast the cake on the barbecue or under a broiler on both sides.

To serve, place a slice of cake on a plate, scoop some ice cream on, top with figs, and dust with a little confectioners' sugar, for that special "new-fallen snow" effect!

Barbecued figs on toasted fruit cake with ice cream

Banana and Gingernut cheesecake with lime and clove cream

This is my partner, Michael McGrath's, best baked cheesecake recipe, and we've been serving it at The Providores to much praise. The bananas and Gingernut biscuits give it a really delicious edge.

Serves 8 to 10

> 2 to 3 large ripe bananas
>
> 9 oz Gingernut biscuits *or* any hard ginger cookies, finely crushed
>
> $^1/_2$ cup (1 stick) unsalted butter, melted
>
> 1 teaspoon ground cloves
>
> 1$^3/_4$ cups cream cheese
>
> 1$^3/_4$ cups ricotta
>
> 1$^1/_3$ cups superfine sugar
>
> 4 large eggs plus 1 extra white
>
> $^1/_4$ cup (4 tablespoons) butter, melted and cooled

Preheat oven to 350°F. Place unpeeled bananas on a baking sheet and roast until softened and slightly blackened, about 15 minutes. Peel and measure them—you need 2 cups of cooked banana.

Meanwhile, line the base of a 10-inch springform cake pan with parchment paper. Combine Gingernuts, butter, and cloves and press firmly into base.

In a large bowl beat cream cheese with banana. Beat in ricotta and sugar, then eggs and extra egg white, one at a time. Beat in butter until just combined. Pour mixture into pan. Bake 1 hour, turn off the heat, and leave in oven another hour. Cover with plastic wrap and refrigerate for at least 5 hours.

An hour before serving, remove cake from pan and spread the lime and clove cream on top. Return to the fridge for an hour before serving.

Lime and clove cream

> 1$^2/_3$ cups heavy cream
>
> finely grated zest and juice of 2 limes
>
> $^1/_2$ teaspoon ground cloves
>
> 1 tablespoon confectioners' sugar

Whip cream with all other ingredients to form moderately firm peaks.

Layered stone fruit crumble with chile salsa

Layered stone fruit crumble with chile salsa

I often think that the crumble you eat from the fridge the day after is more appealing than one straight from the oven. This recipe is for a layered crumble to be eaten cold on a warm day. It has a salsa served with it; really it's just an intriguing extra to make the flavors stand out a bit more—especially as the chile will highlight the sweetness of the fruit. It's great served with cream mixed with a little vanilla.

Serves 6

2 lb mixed stone fruits (I used $1^1/_4$ lb nectarines and $^3/_4$ lb plums)

1 cup (2 sticks) butter, cut into $^3/_4$-inch cubes

2 cups flour

$^1/_2$ scant cup superfine sugar

$^1/_2$ teaspoon baking powder

$^1/_2$ small, hot green chile, finely sliced

2 tablespoons light honey

juice of 1 lemon

Preheat oven to 400°F. Halve fruit and remove pits with a small sharp knife. Put $^1/_3$ lb of the fruit to one side and cut remaining pieces in two. Place these in a lightly greased nonreactive roasting dish 8 x 10 inch in one layer and bake 20 minutes.

Place butter, flour, sugar, and baking powder in a food processor and process until it resembles bread-crumbs. Sprinkle over fruit and return to the oven. Bake until golden and crisp, about 35 minutes. Allow to cool completely.

To make the salsa, cut reserved fruit into small pieces and mix with chile, honey, and lemon juice. Allow to develop for 30 minutes.

To serve, scoop spoonfuls of the cooled crumble into small bowls, making a layered effect with the fruit and crunchy topping. Then spoon salsa on top.

warm desserts

On cool autumn or winter days, what can be a better end to a meal than a rich, warm dessert, served with cream, real custard, or ice cream? But don't let weather dictate when you can eat a warm treat. A rich chocolate hazelnut pudding served with vanilla ice cream or mascarpone makes a great end to a meal in summer or winter. Poached fruit can be equally as delicious served all year round. The halva-crusted pear compote is based on something I ate in Turkey in summer, but it is great to eat in winter. The aim of a dessert is to round off a meal without letting your guests get too full, although any really great dessert will have your friends asking for seconds.

Caramelized apple and passion fruit compote

This recipe is a good all-rounder—try it served on pancakes with ice cream, as a topping on grilled brioche with crème fraîche, or simply with some custard. This will keep in a sealed container in the fridge for three to four days, but, because of the butter content, it does need to be warmed a little before you serve it.

Serves 4

4 firm cooking *or* Granny Smith apples, peeled and cored

1/2 cup (1 stick) plus 3 tablespoons unsalted butter

3/4 cup demerara *or* raw sugar

3/4 cup orange juice

6 passion fruits, pulp removed

Peel and core apples and cut each one into sixths. Put butter and sugar into a deep-sided saucepan and slowly melt, stirring until sugar is dissolved. Turn the heat up and cook until it caramelizes—you will begin to smell this change, and the color will deepen.

Add apple segments to sugar mixture and stir gently, being careful not to burn yourself. Add orange juice and bring to a boil, cover, and simmer until apples are almost cooked, but not breaking up.

Lastly, add passion fruit, simmer another minute, then remove from heat and it's ready.

Caramelized apple and passion fruit compote

Chocolate hazelnut puddings

These were a firm favorite at the original Sugar Club restaurant in Wellington, New Zealand, over eighteen years ago. I've worked on improving the recipe since then, and I still like to make them as much now as then. They're lovely served with a dollop of mascarpone on top, then cream poured over that.

Serves 6

$1/2$ cup (1 stick) unsalted butter (plus extra for greasing ramekins)

$1/2$ cup superfine sugar (plus extra for dusting ramekins)

4 oz dark chocolate, roughly chopped

$2/3$ cup flour

$1/3$ cup cocoa

$1/2$ cup soft fresh breadcrumbs

$3/4$ cup hazelnuts, roasted, peeled, and roughly chopped

5 eggs, separated

1 teaspoon pure vanilla extract

Preheat oven to 350°F. Lightly butter six 1-cup ovenproof ramekins. Coat with sugar and pour out the excess. Make a bain-marie by placing a roasting dish on a shelf in the middle of the oven and pouring in boiling water to a depth of $1^1/4$ inches.

Put butter, chocolate, and half the sugar in a heatproof bowl and melt over a saucepan of simmering water. Sieve flour and cocoa and mix with breadcrumbs and hazelnuts. Beat egg whites with remaining sugar until firm peaks form. Mix egg yolks and vanilla into chocolate mixture, then stir in flour mixture. Stir one-third of meringue into chocolate mixture, then carefully fold in remaining two-thirds until just combined. Spoon mixture into prepared dishes and place them in the bain-marie. Bake 20 to 30 minutes. Test with a thin knife or skewer pushed into the middle—it should come out clean. Remove bain-marie carefully from the oven and then remove puddings in their ramekins using tongs or carefully using your fingers. Leave for a few minutes before turning out. Serve straight away with either whipped cream or mascarpone. They can also be successfully reheated later in a microwave.

Palm sugar and ginger coconut cream sauce

I like to serve this drizzled over steamed puddings. This is the Pacific Rim cousin of caramel sauce. You can make it up to three days in advance. Coconut palm sugar is sold at Asian food stores. If you can't get any, use a sugar high in molasses such as demerara or brown sugar.

Serves 8

- $1/3$ lb coconut palm sugar, roughly chopped, *or* $3/4$ cup brown sugar
- 1 cup unsweetened coconut cream
- 1 lump candied *or* stem ginger, finely chopped
- 1 cup cream

Place palm sugar and coconut cream in a pan and heat gently until the sugar has melted into the cream. Boil for 1 minute, then add ginger and cream, bring back to a boil, and simmer for 2 minutes.

Amaretti chocolate sauce

This simple sauce can lift the ordinary vanilla ice cream into a treat of a dessert. It's also lovely served alongside a vanilla sponge cake or with poached pears or nectarines.

Serves 6

- $6^1/2$ oz dark chocolate
- $1^1/4$ cups heavy cream, warmed
- 3 tablespoons Amaretto liqueur
- 4 amaretti biscuits *or* bitter almond cookies, roughly crushed

Place chocolate in a heatproof bowl over a pan of simmering water and heat until melted, stirring frequently. Pour in cream and mix well, then stir in liqueur and cookies. Spoon over ice cream, cake, or whatever you feel like eating.

Stephanie Creed's berry cherry apple hazelnut crumble

I first met Stephanie in New Zealand in the late eighties, but she has lived in London for almost ten years now. We've had many meals with Steph, and this was something she threw together one day for us. Her handy hint is "eat this with whipped cream."

Serves 6

- $3/4$ to 1 lb mixture of raspberries, blueberries, blackberries, and boysenberries
- $1^1/2$ cups fresh pitted cherries *or* 1 can pitted black cherries, drained
- 2 large, sour apples, peeled, cored, and finely sliced
- $1^1/3$ cups sugar
- 1 cup (2 sticks) unsalted butter
- $2^1/3$ cups self-rising flour
- $1/2$ cup hazelnuts, toasted, skinned, and ground
- $1/4$ cup (4 tablespoons) extra butter, cut in $1/2$-inch cubes

Preheat oven to 350°F. Mix berries, cherries, and apples together with half the sugar. Place in a greased $9^1/2$-inch ovenproof dish. Using a food processor or your fingers, rub butter into flour to resemble breadcrumbs and mix in remaining sugar and hazelnuts. Sprinkle the crumble mixture over fruit and dot with the extra butter. Bake until the crust is golden and the juices begin to seep through.

Cherry and chocolate clafouti

I first made this when I lived in an old wooden house in beautiful Karaka Bay in Wellington. It was a perfect dish for those days, placed on the old kauri table, which looked out over the harbor, and served at a leisurely pace. Serve it warm with a little cream or vanilla ice cream. Black cherries give the best result.

Serves 8

2 tablespoons unsalted butter, to grease the dish

$3/4$ to 1 lb ripe cherries, washed and pitted, *or* canned pitted black cherries, well drained

1 heaping cup flour

$1/2$ teaspoon baking powder

$1/2$ cup superfine sugar

4 eggs

$12/3$ cups milk

$1/4$ cup kirsch (optional)

5 oz bitter chocolate, coarsely chopped or grated

$1/4$ cup confectioners' sugar

Preheat oven to 375°F and place a baking sheet in the upper part. Grease a 6-cup ceramic dish with butter and scatter cherries in evenly. Sift flour and baking powder into a bowl and whisk in half the sugar. Make a well in the center.

Beat eggs with remaining sugar, then whisk in half the milk. Pour this mixture into the well and beat until you have a lump-free batter. Beat in remaining milk, kirsch, and chocolate.

Pour the batter over cherries and place in the oven. Bake until the batter is golden on top and cooked through, about 30 minutes. Test with a skewer—it should come out clean (although the chocolate will stick a little to the skewer). Take from the oven and dredge liberally with confectioners' sugar.

Banana and coconut tarts

These little tarts are truly delicious, and the only thing I will stipulate is that the bananas are ripe—if they're a little green they won't caramelize and the rich flavor will be lost. You can also add a little spice if you wish; some allspice or nutmeg mashed into the bananas works really well. These are a good dinner party dessert as you can have them sitting on the baking sheet, brushed with butter in the fridge, then just throw them in the oven as you clear the main course. Serve warm with runny cream or ice cream.

Makes 4

   1 sheet puff pastry, thawed

   6 ripe bananas, peeled

   1 cup shredded coconut

   1/4 cup (4 tablespoons) butter, melted

   2 tablespoons superfine sugar

Preheat oven to 400°F. On a lightly floured cutting board, unfold pastry sheet and cut four 4-inch rounds. Place these on a greased tray and let rest at room temperature for 20 minutes.

Mash two bananas with coconut and spread evenly over pastry. Slice remaining bananas on a slight angle, about 1/4 inch thick, and lay on top. Lightly brush pastry and banana with half the butter and sprinkle with sugar.

Bake in the middle of the oven until pastry is golden and bananas are lightly caramelized, about 15 minutes. Brush the remaining butter over the tarts and bake another 2 to 3 minutes.

Pear, pistachio, and ginger compote with grilled halva crust

This is based on a simple pudding of grilled halva and walnuts that Michael and I ate in the seaside Turkish village of Gumuslik with our friends Tarik and Savas, who own the restaurant changa in Istanbul. This compote is great served with whipped cream and a crisp cookie (like Changa Nut Shortbread, page 172).

Serves 6

   4 large pears, peeled, cored, and diced

   $1/2$ teaspoon ground cinnamon

   3 teaspoons finely chopped candied ginger

   $2/3$ cup sugar

   3 tablespoons water

   $3/4$ cup unsalted shelled pistachio nuts, lightly
      toasted

   $2/3$ lb ($10^1/2$ oz) plain halva

Place pears, cinnamon, ginger, and all but two teaspoons of the sugar into a saucepan. Add water, cover, and slowly bring to a boil. Simmer until pears are cooked, but still a little firm. Cool, then mix in nuts and spoon into six ovenproof dishes or one large dish, making the top as level as possible. This can be done a few hours in advance.

Crumble or grate halva and spread it evenly over the pear mixture, making it level as well. Sprinkle remaining sugar on top, then grill (either under an overhead broiler or using a cook's blowtorch) until sugar and halva begin to darken. (Watch carefully, as halva will darken quite quickly. It's best to grill under a moderate heat.) Stand for a minute before eating, as the caramel will be fiercely hot.

Ginger butter and honey roasted feijoas

In New Zealand, feijoas arrive in the marketplace in massive quantities during their short growing season, when they all ripen at the same time. A native of South America, and often called "pineapple guava," they have taken to New Zealand's climate with a vigor. The ones we found in London came mainly from their native South America, but I was craving the ones from back home, which are richer and more aromatic. Anyway, I made the following, and it made me homesick.

Serves 4

   $1/2$ 2-day-old white loaf, crusts removed, cut into
      $3/4$-inch cubes

   $1/2$ cup (1 stick) plus 3 tablespoons butter

   8 medium feijoas, peeled

   2 small knobs candied or stem ginger, coarsely grated

   $1/2$ scant cup light honey

   juice of 1 very juicy and ripe lemon

   vanilla ice cream to serve

Preheat oven to 325°F. Place bread in a food processor and process to produce coarse crumbs (or you could grate it on a coarse grater). Place 4 tablespoons of the butter in an ovenproof frying pan and heat over a moderate heat until bubbling. Add breadcrumbs and toss continuously until golden and crisp. Transfer to paper towels to cool.

Wipe out pan and place it back on the heat. Add remaining butter and melt. Add feijoas and cook for 1 minute over a moderate heat, turning continuously. Add ginger and honey and bring to a boil, then add lemon juice and bake for 15 minutes. Remove and leave to rest for a few minutes before sprinkling with breadcrumbs and serving with a scoop or two of vanilla ice cream.

Apple, amaretti, mascarpone, and chocolate pies

Yummy is the only way to describe these pies. They are best served warm, with plenty of thick clotted cream or crème fraîche and a glass of Amaretto.

Makes 4

3 puff pastry sheets, thawed

1 egg, lightly beaten

2 medium Granny Smith apples, peeled, cored, and halved horizontally

3¹/₂ oz mascarpone

4 amaretti biscuits *or* bitter almond cookies

3¹/₂ oz bitter chocolate, grated

6 tablespoons demerara *or* raw sugar

Preheat oven to 400°F. Lightly grease a baking sheet. On a lightly floured work surface, unfold pastry sheets. Cut one sheet in half and attach to other pastry sheets to form two large rectangles. Cut each rectangle in half widthwise to create four equal pieces, and brush each piece all over with beaten egg. Place an apple half, cut side down, at one end of each piece of pastry. Dollop a quarter of the mascarpone on each piece of apple, place an amaretti biscuit on top, then spinkle with chocolate and 1 tablespoon of the sugar. Fold pastry over the apple, gently squeezing out any air, and press down well. Cut into a circular shape with a sharp knife. Repeat to make four pies. Brush pies with remaining egg wash and sprinkle with remaining sugar. Poke a few holes in top with a toothpick and bake for 30 minutes, until puffed and golden.

Pear, quince, and chocolate pizzas

A Japanese food magazine that I have occasionally written for once asked me if I had ever made a dessert pizza, which may seem an unusual idea at first, but really a pizza is just a carbohydrate base with a topping (think of it like a flat tart). Many years ago I did make a dessert pizza, and this is it—a real taste treat. The base is a variation of brioche, a sweet yeast bread enriched with butter and eggs.

Serves 6

1 teaspoon active dried yeast

3 tablespoons tepid milk

^{1}/$_2$ scant cup brown sugar

1 egg plus 2 yolks

2 cups flour

pinch salt

^{1}/$_2$ cup (1 stick) plus 3 tablespoons butter, softened but not melted

5 oz bitter chocolate, roughly chopped

3 pears, cores removed and cut into 8 wedges each

3^1/$_2$ oz quince paste, cut into ^{1}/$_4$-inch cubes

Dissolve yeast in the milk with 2 teaspoons of the brown sugar and leave in a warm place. When it begins to froth, whisk in the egg and yolks.

Sift flour with salt and remaining brown sugar and put three-quarters of it into a bowl. Add the yeast mixture and bring together either by hand or with a dough hook.

Add butter in four equal batches, mixing well between each addition. Knead in remaining flour mixture. Cover bowl with plastic wrap and leave in a warm place until doubled in size—about 1 hour.

Punch dough down with your fist and knead briefly, then divide into six balls. Press each ball between your hands to make a disk about 4 inches in diameter. Place on a lightly buttered baking sheet.

Divide chocolate between bases, then pear wedges, and lastly quince paste. Leave in a warm spot for 10 minutes. Pre-heat the oven to 400°F. Place pizzas on the middle shelf and bake until the bases are golden and crusty and the tops start to brown, about 20 minutes.

Apple, amaretti, and cardamom crumble

I like to make this in individual ramekins and serve it with scoops of vanilla ice cream on top and a drizzle of Amaretto liqueur.

Serves 6

8 slightly sour apples (like Granny Smith), peeled and cored

1 teaspoon ground cardamom

$^1/_2$ scant cup sugar

18 amaretti biscuits *or* bitter almond cookies

$^1/_2$ teaspoon vanilla extract

$^3/_4$ cup (1$^1/_2$ sticks) unsalted butter

1$^1/_3$ cups self-rising flour

Preheat oven to 350°F. Cut apples into eighths and place in a pan with cardamom and half the sugar. Bring slowly to a simmer and cook with a lid on until apples are almost cooked and slightly mushy.

Crumble amaretti cookies in your hand and add a third of them to apples with the vanilla and mix well. Divide between six ramekins.

Melt a walnut-sized piece of butter and set aside. Place remaining butter in a food processor (or you can do this next bit by hand) with flour and remaining sugar and process into crumbs, then transfer to a bowl and mix with remaining crumbled amaretti biscuits. Sprinkle this crumble topping over stewed apple and gently press down, then drizzle with melted butter. Place ramekins onto a baking sheet in the middle of the oven and bake until the topping is golden and crunchy. Serve straight from the oven.

Banana, apple, and crunchy sesame pudding

This simple pudding is delicious with whipped cream or vanilla ice cream. Actually, now I think of it, every pudding is made even more delicious with cream or ice cream! I tend to use Granny Smiths or a similarly tart apple.

Serves 6 to 8

$^1/_4$ cup ($^1/_2$ stick) unsalted butter

4 ripe bananas, peeled and cut into $^3/_4$-inch pieces

4 large apples, cored and cut into thumb-thick wedges

juice of 1 large, juicy lemon

1 cup demerara *or* soft brown sugar

4 teaspoons sesame seeds, toasted

Heat half the butter in a 12-inch frying pan with a heatproof handle. When it begins to turn nut-brown, add sliced bananas and fry for 1 minute over a high heat, tossing occasionally.

Transfer bananas to a bowl, add remaining butter to the pan, and return to the heat.

Cook apple wedges in the same way, but for 2 minutes. Add lemon juice and $^1/_3$ cup of the sugar to the pan, toss well, and cook until sugar begins to caramelize.

Return bananas to the pan, press flat, and sprinkle with sesame seeds and remaining sugar. Place under a hot broiler and cook until sugar caramelizes.

Allow to cool for 2 minutes before serving.

(Photograph of recipe on page 2.)

Vanilla roasted plums with basil mascarpone

I admit to a fondness for roasting fruit; it intensifies the flavor and texture. This recipe works well with all stone fruits, although the cooking time may vary. As for the basil mascarpone, you'll just have to try it.

Serves 4

$^1/_2$ **vanilla bean, split in half lengthways** *or*

$^1/_2$ **teaspoon natural vanilla extract**

8 large plums, halved and pits removed

$^3/_4$ **cup superfine sugar**

1 cup sweet white wine

Preheat oven to 400°F. Place vanilla on the bottom of a baking dish, preferably ceramic, just large enough to hold all the fruit in one layer. Mix plums with half the sugar, then place on top of vanilla, cut sides up. Drizzle wine over the plums and sprinkle with remaining sugar. Bake 20 to 30 minutes. Plums are cooked when they begin to caramelize on top and start to soften inside. Remove from oven and let cool in the dish, or serve straight away while still warm.

Basil mascarpone

$3^1/_2$ **oz mascarpone**

8 basil leaves, finely sliced

2 tablespoons superfine sugar

$^2/_3$ **cup heavy** *or* **whipping cream**

Place mascarpone, basil, and sugar in a bowl and whisk briefly to bruise the basil. Add cream and whip to form soft peaks. Serve a good dollop of this with the plums.

Baked rhubarb with lemon grass and cloves

Rhubarb has such great attributes for a variety of desserts—it's not naturally sweet, it has zing, and it goes so well with cream. If you can't find lemon grass, use 1 teaspoon of finely grated lemon zest instead.

Serves 4

1¼ lb rhubarb, cut into 4-inch-long pieces

1 stem lemon grass, bashed flat with a heavy knife or hammer

½ scant cup superfine sugar

1 teaspoon ground cloves

1 scant cup sweet dessert (sticky) wine

Preheat oven to 325°F. Toss together rhubarb, lemon grass, sugar, and cloves in a ceramic roasting dish just large enough to hold them in one layer. Pour wine over and bake until rhubarb is cooked and the wine has reduced by half, about 30 to 40 minutes. Serve warm with whipped cream and a crisp cookie or two.

Nectarines stuffed with pistachios and honey

This is a new take on a classic Italian dessert. Serve nectarines just warm or enjoy them cold at a picnic. For extra flavor, add a few tablespoons of your favorite liqueur to the filling—the excess will drizzle into the finished syrup and make it even better. Peaches are also delicious prepared this way.

Serves 4

4 large, ripe nectarines

½ cup (1 stick) plus 3 tablespoons unsalted butter

1 cup shelled, unsalted pistachio nuts, coarsely chopped

½ scant cup light honey

finely grated zest of 1 lemon

Preheat oven to 350°F. Halve nectarines and remove the pits. Using a teaspoon, scoop out a little of the flesh to allow for more stuffing. Lightly grease a roasting dish with 1 teaspoon of butter and place fruit halves in, cut side up. Bring nuts, honey, remaining butter, and lemon zest to a boil in a small saucepan, stirring slowly. Boil a few minutes until the mixture starts to caramelize, then spoon into the fruit cavities. Bake 20 minutes until nuts start to turn a golden brown. Rest for 15 minutes before serving with dollops of whipped cream.

Nectarines stuffed with pistachios and honey

Creamy poached caramel pears

Creamy poached caramel pears

These pears are very rich and sumptuous. They're good served with toasted pound cake or pannettone, or with a scoop of vanilla ice cream.

Serves 8

- 8 medium-large pears, (remove the core if you wish)
- 2^1/$_3$ cups (1 lb) superfine sugar
- ^{1}/$_3$ cup water
- 1 orange, skin peeled off with a peeler, juiced
- 1 cup hot water
- 1 cup heavy cream

Use a potato peeler to peel the pears in strips to give a striped effect. Place sugar and the ^{1}/$_3$ cup water into a large deep saucepan and bring to a boil, stirring until sugar is dissolved. Once it comes to a boil, remove the spoon and don't stir it again. When the sugar has cooked to a pale caramel, place the pears in, then the orange juice and peel and 1 cup of hot water. Put a lid on the pot and simmer for 15 minutes.

Add cream and continue to cook until pears are tender (a skewer will go through easily). Take the lid off and continue to cook until cream has reduced to a caramel sauce. This will take about 20 minutes, so watch carefully to make sure the toffee does not stick or burn.

Baked pears stuffed with ginger and chocolate ricotta

This is a real autumnal dessert and a favorite of mine on a Sunday afternoon after a roast. I like to eat it with lightly whipped cream, flavored with a little nutmeg and confectioners' sugar.

Serves 6

- 6 medium-large cooking pears
- ^{2}/$_3$ cup fresh ricotta
- 2 pieces crystalized *or* stem ginger, finely chopped
- 3^1/$_2$ oz bitter chocolate, roughly chopped
- ^{1}/$_2$ cup confectioners' sugar
- ^{1}/$_4$ cup (^{1}/$_2$ stick) butter, melted
- 1 scant cup sweet dessert wine

Preheat oven to 350°F. Cut the bottom off each pear, just so that they will stand upright. Peel them if desired. Using a melon baller or apple corer, remove the core and seeds, leaving a space about the size of a large walnut.

Press ricotta through a sieve and mix with ginger, chocolate, and confectioners' sugar. Stuff this mixture inside the pears.

Cut four 4^2/$_3$-inch squares of foil or parchment paper, and brush one side with melted butter. Place one pear upright on each square, then brush with remaining butter. Fold the excess foil or paper around pears, then set in a roasting dish that is just large enough to hold them upright.

Pour wine over and bake 45 to 60 minutes, until a skewer poked into the thickest part of the "neck" passes through easily. Allow to cool for 10 minutes before attempting to remove the foil, then pour reduced wine over and serve.

glossary

Amaretti biscuits are crunchy little Italian cookies, flavored with apricot kernels or bitter almonds.

Amaretto liqueur is a liqueur flavored with apricot kernels or bitter almonds.

Balsamic vinegar actually comes as two types: the more usual Aceto Balsamico and the very expensive and delicious Aceto Balsamico Tradizionale di Modena. Both come from Modena, Italy, and both are made by traditional methods, from Trebbiano grapes, although the former will usually have white wine vinegar added. A good balsamic (and be warned—there are some dubious ones out there) should have a concentrated flavor, residual sugars, and a light acidity.

Black vinegar is used in Chinese cuisine. The better ones are well aged and have a complex smoky flavor; they tend to be sweet, with hints of spice. Mix a little finely grated orange zest into malt vinegar with a pinch of ground allspice and honey for a substitute.

Bok choy is a vegetable with crunchy white stems and leafy leaves. You can eat the whole thing. Great wok-fried with a hint of soy sauce. If you can't locate it, try its cousins: pak choy, choi sum, gai lan, or morning glory.

Boquet garni: This classic of French kitchens was traditionally composed of a bay leaf, thyme, and parsley stalks tied together in a bundle, although nowadays you're likely to find oregano and rosemary, among others, in there as well.

Caperberries, also called "capernuts," are a pickled fruit from the caper bush. The flowers are pickled into capers, but if the flower is allowed to open and become pollinated, then the fruit that grows is what becomes the caperberry. If using for flavor, then use large capers in their place, but if using in salads, you'd be better to have a mixture of salty brined green olives and capers.

Chioca, called "yams" in New Zealand, are a tuberous vegetable native to Peru.

Chorizo is a Spanish sausage and comes in two main forms. One is cured and ready to slice and eat much like an Italian salami; the other is to be cooked, usually grilled or boiled. They have a distinct red color and smoky taste, imparted from the pimentón (smoked paprika) that is added when they're made.

Conchiglie: Large shell-shaped pasta.

Curry leaves (*Murraya koenigii*) are sourced mainly from southern India and have a distinct fresh, nutty taste—they don't taste of curry powder (which derives most of its flavor from fenugreek). They freeze well for a few months, stored in an airtight bag. Curry leaves have a flavor all of their own; if you can't find them use torn kaffir lime leaves as a replacement.

Demerara sugar is a high-molasses sugar used regularly in British cookery. Substitute it with turbinado or other raw sugar or packed brown sugar.

Enoki (*Flammulina velutipes*) are small Japanese mushrooms on long slender stems that grow in clusters.

Galangal is a relative of ginger, but more "raw tasting" and very aromatic. Called "blue ginger" in Chinese. This can be replaced with fresh ginger, but it won't give you the exact flavor. Try to find freeze-dried ground galangal powder, sometimes called "laos."

Golden syrup is a sweet golden syrup, much like corn syrup, but containing natural sugar molasses. Replace it with maple syrup or corn syrup with brown sugar.

Herbs (hard and soft): I use these terms to differentiate herbs. In the former I would include rosemary, sage, thyme, oregano, and bay. In the latter: basil, mint, tarragon, parsley, and cilantro. Hard herbs can cope with cooking, but soft herbs often benefit from being added at the end of the cooking process or not cooked at all.

Hoisin is a thick, slightly sweet and spicy sauce made from fermented soy beans.

Hummus is a creamy dip made from puréed chickpeas, olive oil, lemon juice, garlic, and sesame-seed paste (see *Tahini*).

Jicama (also called "yam bean") is a large spinning top–shaped tuber with crispy white flesh. Look for it at Asian and South American vegetable sections or markets. A combination of crisp apple and celeriac may be used as a substitute in salads.

Kaffir lime leaves are used for flavoring, much like bay leaves, but taste of lime. From the kaffir lime tree, which produces a knobbly, not very juicy fruit. The leaves can also be very finely shredded and added to dishes and eaten. Freshly grated lime zest can be used as a substitution.

Kirmizi biber are Turkish chile flakes. These are more oily, less raw tasting, and smell more lovely than regular dry chile flakes, although you can interchange both.

Kohlrabi (*Brassica oleraccea*) is an unusual looking vegetable resembling a turnip with lots of leafy shoots coming off the bulb. Grate it raw and add to coleslaw or other salads or cook it briefly by steaming or boiling, but don't overcook it. Use jicama as a replacement in raw or lightly cooked dishes, or turnips in cooked dishes, although they have a more noticeable flavor, so use slightly less of them.

Kumara is New Zealand's native sweet potato, although it was actually brought across the Pacific by the Maori over 500 years ago. You can substitute sweet potatoes or yams.

Kumquat is a sour fruit, which looks like a Lilliput orange, although the seeds are almost as large as in an orange. They need to be cooked with lots of sugar. Makes a great marmalade, if you can be bothered taking the seeds out. Sometimes spelled cumquat.

Laksa is the name given to a variety of fantastic soups from Malaysia and Singapore, although it's far more than just a soup. It will always contain noodles of some description, be spicy to very spicy, sometimes made from coconut milk, always delicious.

Manuka honey is one of New Zealand's most delicious and iconic treats. It's not only good eaten spread thick on toast and muffins, but also great in baking and barbecue glazes, and it has a reputation for helping calm stomach aches and disorders. Use a rich dark honey in its place, although better health stores may carry it.

Mascarpone is an Italian soft cheese, most similar to cream cheese, although far richer and smoother. You could use cream cheese at a pinch.

Mirin is a sweetened Japanese sake, made from distilled rice spirit, koji (a yeastlike rice culture), and steamed glutinous rice. Not for drinking, but traditionally used in cooking, although I also use it in dressings.

Miso is a rich savory paste, made from soy beans, koji (see *Mirin*), and often rice, traditionally used in thin soups as a seasoning. There are many grades: from shiro-miso (white miso, sweet and light) through to aka-miso (red and strong tasting). I like to use it as a seasoning in soups and stews; as a marinade on meats, fish and tofu; and in dressings to add body and depth.

Nashi (*Pyrus pyrifolia*) are round apple-shaped pears with yellow skin and crisp, juicy flesh. Also known as "asian pear."

Nigella seeds (*Nigella sativa*) come from a plant of the buttercup family and are often used in North African and Indian cooking. These can be replaced visually with black sesame seeds, but for flavor use a slightly smaller amount of toasted cumin.

Nori is a type of seaweed, also called "laver" by the Welsh. Used in Japanese sushi making to hold rice and flavorings together in a nori roll or California roll. Made much like sheets of homemade paper, the seaweed is pulped, then dried on fine mesh nets to produce fragile paperlike squares.

Orecchiette is a small pasta shaped like an ear.

Pak choy: See *Bok choy*.

Palm sugar is made by tapping the syrup from a few varieties of palm tree, just the same way that maple syrup is collected. It is then boiled over slow fires to reduce the liquid content and then set in molds. It has a slightly burnedmolasses taste to it, but is quite fantastic. Look for it in Asian markets. You can substitute brown sugar in a pinch.

Pancetta is Italian pork belly, cured and sometimes rolled. Treat it much like bacon, although it's much firmer in texture. In Spain they have something called panceta, which is usually slablike rather than rolled, but used in much the same way.

Paprika: There are many types; the most famous are produced in Hungary and Spain. The former is often smooth, spicy, and sweet; the latter is either one or the other. In Spain they have *pimentón dulce* (sweet) and *pimentón picante* (spicy), which are smoked paprikas, made by drying the peppers over gently smoking wood.

Pepitas: Pumpkin seeds.

Polenta is a type of grainy yellow cornmeal.

Pomegranate molasses is an astringent-sweet syrup made from reduced pomegranate juice. Found throughout the

Middle East, from Turkey to Lebanon, it has an almost addictive quality. Honey mixed with lemon juice and balsamic vinegar would be the nearest you could get as a replacement.

Porcini (*Boletus edulis*) are creamy-brown mushrooms. Their name literally means "little piglets."

Rice vinegar is a vinegar made, not surprisingly, from rice! Although it is sometimes the case that other grains are included as well. Japanese rice vinegar is usually weaker in acidity than, for example, white vinegar (usually made from grapes), so make sure you taste the finished dish and check the taste.

Risotto rice is a special type of Italian rice that has been bred for this one particular dish. The three main types of risotto rice are Arborio, Carnaroli, and Vialone Nana.

Saffron is the world's most expensive spice. It comes from the stamens of a particular crocus. It adds a rich golden color to dishes and a distinctive but indescribable flavor. Best to use it subtly rather than overpoweringly—the flavor is really quite strong. Threads are superior to powder, but both will give you similar results.

Sake is a spirit made from fermented rice, koji (see *Mirin*), and water. It is the national drink of Japan, highly revered and strong. Available from good bottle stores, Japanese shops, and some Asian markets.

Scallops vary the world over, from small Queen scallops to the scallops we serve at The Providores restaurant in London—massive diver caught Scottish creatures that come complete with the coral attached—the red-orange "tongue" that forms part of the meat. If you are lucky enough to find scallops with the coral still on (it's sometimes removed when they are shelled), then do cook it. The flesh of scallops is incredibly rich and sweet, and the coral provides a wonderful contrast, as it has a very slight bitterness and creaminess.

Sherry vinegar is a rich-tasting, lightly acidic aromatic vinegar made from Spanish sherry. It's usually used in salad dressings, marinades, or for deglazing pans. Available from gourmet markets and larger supermarkets.

Star anise is a seed pod from a tree native to Southern China. It is, not surprisingly, star shaped! It is the star, not the seeds that it contains, that gives the flavor. The flavor is like sweet woody aniseed. You can find it in any Chinatown, larger supermarkets, and Asian food shops.

Squash are a family of vegetables, often interchangable with pumpkin, that include butternut, kuri, acorn, spaghetti (the flesh looks like a gelatinous spaghetti), and many others.

Sumac is a berry from a shrub found in the Middle East, mostly ground to a coarse powder. It has an astringent quality, much like tamarind, and is usually sprinkled onto the finished dish in countries from Israel through to Syria and Turkey.

Tahini is a creamy paste made from ground sesame seeds. Used throughout the Middle East, the Aegean, and Japan, versions of it are sold by supermarkets and health food shops. In Japan they produce the regular pale variety and a strangely delicious black version, made from black unhulled sesame seeds. The latter makes great ice creams.

Tamari is a superior, wheat-free soy sauce; it can be substituted with good quality shoyu (regular soy sauce).

Tamarind is a beautiful tree that thrives in Southeast Asia and India, producing a brown bean podlike fruit. Inside the pod are a sticky brown paste, fibers, and seeds. It's usually sold as slabs of paste, as a strained paste, or as a thick sticky black purée. Look in the international section of your supermarket or in Asian food shops. To obtain tamarind water, soak a walnut-sized chunk of the fibrous paste in 1 cup hot water until soft; squeeze the pulp between your fingers, then strain. This liquid can then be frozen in ice-cube trays for later use. Pomegranate molasses is a good substitutes although it will be sweeter than tamarind. Lime juice is also another way to sour a dish.

Tapenade is a paste made from pureéd or chopped pitted olives. Often capers, olive oil, garlic, and even anchovies may be added for extra character.

Thai fish sauce is also called "nam pla." It's made from fermented fish and is widely used in Thai cooking. Despite its dreadful and distinctive smell, it can become an almost addictive flavor enhancer and tastes nothing like it smells. Trust me.

Wasabi is a mountain hollyhock that will only grow in the purest fresh water. Often referred to as Japanese horseradish, although they're not related. The root is hard to come by, so you'll usually find it as a powder or a paste. It is often mixed with regular horseradish to boost its heat when sold commercially. It will also clear your sinuses rather violently if too much is eaten at once or if you confuse it for a ball of mashed avocado on your sushi plate! Be warned—it is fiery!

index